FINDING

University of Nebraska Press
Lincoln and London

FINDING THE CENTER

NARRATIVE POETRY OF THE ZUNI INDIANS
TRANSLATED BY **DENNIS TEDLOCK**

FROM PERFORMANCES IN THE ZUNI BY ANDREW PEYNETSA AND WALTER SANCHEZ

Preface to the Bison Book Edition Copyright © 1978 by the University of Nebraska Press

Copyright © 1972 by Dennis Tedlock

First Bison Book printing: 1978

Most recent printing indicated by first digit below:

     5   6   7   8   9   10

Library of Congress Cataloging in Publication Data

Tedlock, Dennis, 1939–
   Finding the center.

   "Bison book edition."
   Reprint of the ed. published by Dial Press, New York; with new pref.
   Includes bibliographies.
   1. Zuñi poetry—Translations into English.   2. American poetry—Translations from Zuñi.   I.   Title.
PM2711.Z95E5   1978   897.4   78–9611
ISBN 0–8032–4401–0
ISBN 0–8032–9400–X pbk.

∞

Published by arrangement with the author

Manufactured in the United States of America

Illustrations adapted from The Rain Bird, *by* Harry P. Mera, *courtesy of the School of American Research, Santa Fe*

Special acknowledgment is due Joseph Peynetsa, who assisted in the making of the translations, and provided invaluable comments which appear throughout the notes.

Hom aaky'asse
aawan ts'inaawe.

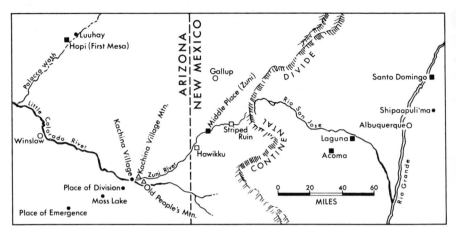

MAPS OF THE ZUNI REGION
Showing Places Mentioned in the Narratives

KEY (both maps)

- ■ Present-day Pueblo Indian village
- □ Ruin of Pueblo Indian village
- ○ Non-Indian town
- △ Hill or Mountain
- ● other location

NOTE: Many locations are only approximate

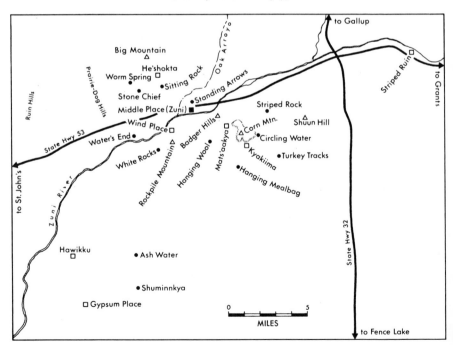

Contents

THE BEGINNING

Preface to the Bison Book Edition

This is still the only book devoted to detailed scores for oral narrative performances, complete with the original pauses, shouts, whispers, chants, and changing tones of voice. The present narratives are translated from the Zuni language of New Mexico, but the same mode of presentation could be a vehicle for any other spoken tradition.[1] I see the book in part as a contribution to the ongoing reopening of the ear and voice that Charles Olson called for all the way back in 1950, when he said that poetry must "catch up and put into itself certain laws and possibilities of the breath."[2] The reopening of the possibilities in our own language goes hand in hand, or voice in voice, with a new openness to the spoken words of other traditions, especially those that spring from the same continent where we are now learning, however slowly, how to become natives.

I hope that at least some of the readers of this book will be people who do not ordinarily find themselves in the midst of a book of poetry. The poets presented here respect the mysterious qualities of what they have to tell, but they do not set obscurity as a goal. And poetry, in the sense I understand the word here, is not the silent lyrics to imaginary songs: it is just people talking, making speeches and telling stories.[3] That is what the word meant in Chaucer's time, before Wordsworth confused it with verse, and that is what it may come to mean again.

By this time I have heard how various people fared when they tried reading these stories aloud. When Andrew Peynetsa's eldest son Dennis first received a copy of the book, he spent the evening reading "The Beginning" to his family, only he did it *in the Zuni language*; he found the translation to be reversible, line by line, except for my reference to "ozone." For the non-Zuni who wishes to try his or her own hand at the Zuni language, the translation of "Coyote and Junco" is accompanied by a facing-page Zuni text; instructions for pronunciation are included below in the "Guide to Reading Aloud." The only advice I have with regard to the English translations, in addition to what is given in the "Guide," is this: try to sound like someone telling a story, not like someone reciting an elocution lesson, and keep your pace slow and deliberate enough for your listener and for your own sense of the story.

I have been asked why I didn't publish a tape or disc, rather than a book. But I like telling these stories over and over, not once and for all "for the record"; they never come out the same way twice. And I like the picture of readers using their own voices rather than sitting passively before a machine. Anyone who wishes to hear the original performances in the Zuni language will find the tapes on deposit in the library of the American Philosophical Society in Philadelphia, and there is an issue of *Alcheringa* with an insert disc recording of a new story by Andrew Peynetsa, accompanied by an English libretto.[4] Meanwhile, try your voice, even if your purpose is to "study" the stories. That is what "studying" a text originally meant in English: to read it aloud.

The formal opening and closing lines of the telapnaawe or "tales" in this book (the first seven narratives) were left untranslated, but I now have some idea as to what these lines may have meant before long use transformed them into their present forms, rounded and diminished like river pebbles. The first part of the opening, Son'ahchi or So'nahchi, may once have been something like, S ho'na ahhachi, "Now we are taking it up," with the -ch- indicating a repetitive action. It is as if the story had been left lying somewhere and were being picked up again, piece by piece. In the second part of the opening, Sonti inoote, only the first word is a mystery, the second one meaning "long ago"; the full line may once have been something like, S onati inoote, "Now it begins to be made long ago." What we are about to hear, then, is a re-enactment of how the story came into being, how it came to be lying where it lies. In fact, the very next lines will give us the names of the places where the events took place. The closing line, Lee semkonikya, may have been shortened from, Lessi semme konikya, "Enough, the word was short," in which se- is an archaic stem appearing in modern Zuni only in the term selhasshi, "old word," which refers to talk that has been handed down, including all of the ten narratives presented here.

When Barbara Tedlock and I were on one of our periodic return visits to Zuni in 1972, just before this book appeared, Andrew Peynetsa was seized by the idea of creating a new tale out of some surprising recent events that had taken place in his own family.[5] Tales are supposed to take place long ago, but now it was as if Andrew were taking literally the present tense of the formal opening, "Now it begins to be made." When he had finished telling the events that made his new tale, he went on, without breaking the narrative stream, to tell how the participants in those events had sat around in the evening and decided to make up a tale about them, which of course is what had been happening as we all sat there. Toward the close, where he would ordinarily have told us that the tale was the origin of some present-day custom, he said instead, "A story was made!" The moment he finished, his grandsons wanted to show us the evidence of the thirteen-point buck that figured in the story, but when they went outside to get the antlers they discovered a brilliant display of northern lights, almost unheard of as far south as Zuni. We all went outside to look. The cosmos itself had moved in synchrony with Andrew's act of creation.

Andrew Peynetsa and Walter Sanchez both estimated their year of birth as 1904; Walter died in 1972. When we saw Andrew in the winter of 1976, on our way to a year with the Quiché Maya of Guatemala, he was in a quiet, reflective mood, and each morning by the stove he gave us serious talks on the subject of medicine. On the last morning he taught us how to cure a bad fright we had just received out on the highway. We first learned of his death from a Quiché diviner, who gave us the meaning of the disturbing dreams we had both had on the same night. Andrew was my greatest teacher of the powers of the spoken word. As Charles Olson once said, "He who can tell the story right has actually not only given you something, but has moved you on your own narrative."

NOTES

1 For an application to Yucatec Maya narratives, see Allan F. Burns's work in *Alcheringa*, o.s. 4 (1972), 97–103; o.s. 5 (1973), 101–5; n.s. 1, no. 1 (1975), 99–107; n.s. 3, no. 1 (1977), 134–36.

2 "Projective Verse," in *Charles Olson: Human Universe and Other Essays*, ed. Donald Allen (New York: Grove, 1967), 51.

3 For some of my own writings and talks on this and related issues, see "Pueblo Literature: Style and Verisimilitude," in *New Perspectives on the Pueblos*, ed. Alfonso Ortiz (Albuquerque: University of New Mexico Press, 1972), 219–42; "Learning to Listen: Oral History as Poetry," *Boundary 2*, 3 (1975), 707–26; "Toward a Restoration of the Word in the Modern World," *Alcheringa*, n.s. 2, no. 2 (1976), 120–32; "From Prayer to Reprimand," in *Language in Religious Practice*, ed. William J. Samarin (Rowley, Mass.: Newbury House, 1976), 72–83; and "Toward an Oral Poetics," *New Literary History*, 8 (1977), 507–19.

4 "The Story of How a Story Was Made," *Alcheringa*, o.s. 5 (1973), 120–25. Other narratives which do not appear in the present book are Andrew Peynetsa's "When the Old Timers Went Deer Hunting," *Alcheringa*, o.s. 3 (1971), 76–81, and Walter Sanchez's "The Girl and the Protector," *Alcheringa* n.s. 1, no. 1 (1975), 110–50.

5 See the first item in note 4.

Introduction

The Aashiwi, as they call themselves, or the Zuni Indians,[1] live in western New Mexico. They are one of twenty separate groups of Pueblo (village) Indians stretching from Taos in northern New Mexico to Hopi in northeastern Arizona. Their language is unrelated to those spoken by the other Pueblos, and in fact has no clear relationship with any other American Indian language.

The land of the Zunis is a high, rugged plateau, broken by red and yellow sandstone mesas; most of it is covered by low brush or open woods of juniper and piñon (nut pine), but there are ponderosa pine forests in the higher elevations and small irrigated farms in the valleys. When the Spanish arrived in 1539, the Zunis made their living by growing corn, squash, and beans, by gathering more than a hundred species of wild plants, and by hunting deer and smaller game. After the coming of the Spanish they added wheat, chili, and peaches to their crops and began raising stock, primarily sheep. Today their income derives largely from wage work, handicrafts (especially silversmithing), and livestock. They are now more numerous than at any time in their recorded history, with a population of over 6,000.

During the sixteenth century the Zunis lived in six different villages, which the Spanish called "The Seven Cities of Cibola"; by 1630 they had come together in the single village where most of them live today, Shiwina, or "Zuni," also called Halonaawa, "Red Ant Place," or Itiwana, "The Middle Place." Their social structure is exceedingly complex, involving twelve matrilineal

clans, thirteen medicine societies (organizations with secret cur-
ing powers), a masked dance society into which all males are
initiated, a series of hereditary rain-bringing priesthoods whose
highest-ranking members form the religious government of the
village, a secular government of elected officials, four mission
churches, three public schools, a crafts cooperative, and a small
factory.[2]

I first went to Zuni in December of 1958 to attend the
famous Sha'lako ceremony.[3] I returned to do anthropological
field work in November of 1964 and continued until January of
1966; this work was done with the permission of two successive
heads of the Zuni civil government, Fred Bowannie and Robert
Lewis. My principal interest was in oral narratives and their social
and psychological contexts, an interest which had been encour-
aged by John L. Fischer and Munro S. Edmonson of Tulane
University.

Formal Zuni narratives are performed largely by men, and
almost any man over fifty knows at least a few of them. They are
told in the home, where television is now supplanting them, and
in medicine society meetings. They fall into two main categories:
telapnaawe, or "tales," which are regarded as fiction; and stories
of the chimiky'ana'kowa, or "The Beginning," which are re-
garded as historical truth. There are other, less formal narratives
(not represented here) which fall outside these two categories,
including accounts of historical events which are more recent than
"The Beginning."

Telapnaawe, including the first seven narratives in this book,
may be told only from October to March, lest the narrator be
bitten by a snake, and only at night, lest the sun set early. Anyone
who falls asleep during a telapnanne or who fails to stand up and
stretch at the end of such a story may become a hunchback.
Telapnaawe are "fictional" in the same limited sense that our own
fiction is, which is to say that they may contain many realistic

details and may even be based on "true" stories. Among the stories in the present collection, this ambiguity is strongest in "The Sun Priest and the Witch-Woman," which is regarded as "true" in almost every detail and yet is given the opening and closing formulas and other stylistic features of a telapnanne.

Stories of "The Beginning," represented here by the last two narratives in the book, may be told at any season of the year and at any time of day. When told in a ritual context they are chanted; the present examples, told as they were in a hearthside context, contain only a few chanted lines and make less use of esoteric language than ritual versions. The remaining story in this book, "The Shumeekuli," would fit neatly into the early portion of Part II of "The Beginning," but its narrator chose to present it as a separate story, though he himself regards it as part of "The Beginning."

Andrew Peynetsa and Walter Sanchez, the two narrators represented here, were both in their early sixties when their stories were recorded. Related by clan, they are among the few Zunis who still devote a good deal of time to farming. Andrew speaks English but Walter does not. Joseph Peynetsa, who helped in the making of the Zuni transcriptions and English translations of the stories, is Andrew's brother's son. At present he works in the offices of the Zuni government.

I collected nearly a hundred narratives from Andrew and Walter, half of them telapnaawe and the rest having to do with "The Beginning" (only a few of these) or with more recent history. In all instances I used a tape-recorder and had at least one Zuni present other than the narrator himself. The recorder caused no apparent "stage fright"; after all, narrators are "on stage" anyway, with or without a recorder. Andrew and Walter decided for themselves which stories to tell, and in what sequence. The story titles were provided by Andrew, at my request.

Once a story was recorded, Joseph Peynetsa and I faced the

massive task of getting it off the tape and onto paper. Joseph would listen to each Zuni clause or sentence two or three times and then repeat it to me until I was satisfied that my phonetic transcription was accurate; he would then offer a translation which we often discussed or modified before I entered it between the lines of the transcription. As time went on and I acquired more knowledge of the Zuni language, I played an increasingly active role in this process. Our results were good enough as these things go, but linguistic training, with its excessive emphasis on the precise notation of phonemes, had made me deaf to the subtler qualities of the speaking voice, and the tediousness of our work (ten to twenty hours for each hour of tape) made Joseph and myself care less about the precision of the translations than we should have.

When I left the field in 1966 it was already my intention to put together a book of Zuni narratives. At first I saw this task as largely a matter of polishing the rough translations done in the field, but I was unhappy with the flat prose format which had always been used in presenting such narratives. Thinking of Melville Jacobs' suggestion that oral narratives might be better understood as a kind of theater than as an oral equivalent of our own written fiction,[4] and noting that Zuni stories contain many quotations, I considered using a play format, with each quotation labeled according to its speaker and the remaining passages labeled "narrator." But I eventually decided that such a presentation would add nothing, since, in Zuni narratives at least, it is usually perfectly clear which character is responsible for a quotation anyway. Moreover, a play format would divert one's attention from the unitary nature of the storytelling experience: the narrator performs *all* of the roles, not just one of a number of fragmented possibilities, and in a sense he must "identify" with all of them.[5]

I was first led to consider the possibility that Zuni narratives might be poetry by Edmonson's discovery that the *Popol Vuh,* which had always been treated as prose by translators, was composed entirely of couplets.[6] But my search for a similar structure in Zuni stories did not uncover anything which would justify a coupleted format. It was not until late in 1968, after listening to many oral performances of modern poetry, that I returned to my Zuni tapes and began to work out the details of the mode of presentation used here, which combines poetic and dramatic features. The intensive listening involved in such a broad-spectrum translation greatly improved my knowledge of the Zuni language over what it had been in the field, so that I was also able to revise and refine the wording of the original rough translations.

The results of this effort have convinced me that prose has no real existence outside the written page. Narratives of the kind presented here have been labeled and presented as "oral prose" for no better reason than that they are not sung or (in most passages) chanted. Earlier field workers, including my predecessors at Zuni,[7] were hampered in their recognition of the poetic qualities of spoken narratives by the fact that handwritten dictation was their only means of collection. This is a tedious method which involves constant interruptions of the flow of speech and deprives the performer of an attentive native audience. But now that the tape-recorder has become practical and accurate as a field instrument, it is possible to capture true performances and to listen closely, as many times as may be necessary, to all their sounds and silences.

What makes written prose most unfit for representing spoken narrative is that it rolls on for whole paragraphs at a time without taking a breath: there is no silence in it. To solve this problem I have broken Zuni narratives into lines: the shorter pauses, which average three-fourths second and almost never drop below one-half second, are represented here by simple changes of line; the longer pauses, which run from two to three seconds, are represented by strophe breaks. Among the present narratives only two pauses (both about six seconds long) fall outside these two groups; they are represented by spaces markedly larger than the regular strophe breaks.

As a casual inspection of the narratives will show, the punctuation marks and paragraphs of a prose presentation would not be much of a guide to Zuni pauses. Some of the pauses fall between clauses and sentences, but many do not, and some of the clause and sentence boundaries are not accompanied by silence. Even the longer pauses sometimes occur in the midst of a sentence; such pauses help to build the tension in a narrative.

Zuni lines vary constantly in length, ranging from one syllable to more than seventy. In passing from Zuni to English it is possible to at least approximate the original contrasts in line length, as can be seen by comparing the text and translation of "Coyote and Junco."[8] There is no point in preserving exact syllable counts in translation, but radical changes would distort the pace of the narrative. Line length—or, to put it the other way around, the frequency of pauses—is the major cause of variations in the apparent rate at which human speech is delivered: passages with short lines (many pauses) seem slow, while those with long lines (few pauses) seem fast. The rate of syllable articulation, by contrast, plays little role in the speed variations of Zuni or any other language,[9] but there are two occasions in "Pelt Kid and his Grandmother" when the narrator, by deliberate effort, greatly slows his articulation in order to make his words absolutely clear; I have marked these lines *slowly* at the left-hand margin.

Occasionally Zuni word order makes the transposition of lines desirable: in "The Boy and the Deer," for example, a strictly literal treatment would produce some lines like, "Her clothes / she bundled," or "His kinswoman / he beat." It might be argued that the hearer ought to be kept in suspense for a half second as to what the woman is going to do with her clothes or what the man is going to do to his kinswoman, but my sense of the matter is that since "Her clothes / she bundled" sounds like ordinary Zuni, it ought to be transformed into "She bundled / her clothes," which sounds like ordinary English.

The loudness of Zuni narration ranges from just short of a shout to just short of a whisper. Representing this on the page is something of a problem, since most of the devices offered by our writing tradition are ambiguous: an exclamation point, for example, most often indicates something loud, but it is also appropriate after a whispered interjection. My present solution to the problem is to use small type for soft passages or words, larger type for middle-level passages, and capitals for loud passages.

Sometimes middle-level passages are delivered with a heavy stress on the last syllable of each line, as in this example from Part I of "The Beginning":

Kwa' kwa'holh uhsona ho' yu'hetamME.
Ma'homkwat liwan ho'na suWE
Alahho ShiwaNI:
homkwat lukhon ayyu'yaanaky'anNA.

If the meanings of the stressed elements were used as a guide to English translation, the passage would come out something like this:

But I do NOT know about this.
Perhaps our younger broTHER there
the Coral PRIEST:
perhaps he WOULD know.

But the purpose of the stresses in the original passage is not to single out particular *meanings* but to mark off lines. In the words of Joseph Peynetsa, the speaker is "saying it in a way that is not ordinary. He is trying to stress, to bring out an important idea.

It shows authority, and to have a complete thought at the same time, not just trailing off." The following rendition, which emphasizes the line structure, is more appropriate than the one offered above:

But I do not know about THIS.
Perhaps our younger brother THERE
the Coral PRIEST:
perhaps he would KNOW.

The effect of this version does not correspond precisely to anything in English poetry, but it does suggest the stress which is often given to line-ending rhymes.

The important lines in Zuni narrative are sometimes chanted rather than given final stress. As in the following example, most chanted lines are limited to two pitches with an interval of roughly three half tones, and most of them are loud:

TON ^{AA}WAANA TON ^{HE}SHOTAWASHNA

The higher pitches in these two-pitch lines tend to fall on the most important words, so that in this case, unlike that of line-final stress, meaning is an appropriate guide to the arrangement of the translation:

WHEN YOU HAVE ^{GONE} THERE YOU WILL BUILD
HOU_{SES}

Occasionally a chanted line breaks into three pitches, as in this case:

NALHAKNAAWE
               nalhaknaawe
                    nalhaknaawe

Here the interval between the top and bottom pitches runs to about four tones, with the middle pitch closer to the top than to the bottom. The translation is simple:

KILLED THE DEER
killed the deer
killed the deer

It should be noted that the pitches in chanted lines, while far more controlled than those in a normal speaking voice, are not as controlled as in singing.

A long time or distance in Zuni narrative may be indicated by drawing out a vowel sound for two or three seconds while keeping a steady pitch. Thus "akya," "he went," may become "akya———," which seems best in English as "he went o———n." This feature might be represented by repeated vowels rather than by long dashes, but the vagaries of English orthography often preclude that: "ooooooon" would appear to have the same vowel sound as "soon." Lengthened consonants, on the other hand, turn out well as repeated letters: thus Zuni "KY'ALHHHHHH" becomes English "KERSPLASHHHHHH."

Sometimes the lengthening of the Zuni vowel "a" is combined with the control of loudness to produce a crescendo, as in this line:

aaaaaaAAAAAA LHITON IKYA

In this case the repeated vowels have a stronger graphic effect than a long dash, which might work out this way: "a———A." I have kept the "a" in the English versions of such crescendos, but have added an "h" to remind the reader that this is like the vowel in "ah" and not like the one in "bat":

aaaaaaAAAAAAH THE RAIN CAME

Vowel lengthening may also be combined with change of pitch, which produces a glissando:

This is the sound of a person descending a ladder at great speed; I have retained it unchanged in translation.

The special manipulations of voice quality (or tone of voice) in Zuni narrative can be transferred directly into English with no real confusion about the meanings of the affected lines; as in the script for a play, such lines can be introduced with parenthetical, italicized instructions. Sometimes these special voice qualities involve imitations of the voices of the story characters; a boy may be given a *high* voice or, as in the case of the adolescent younger brother Ahayuuta in "The Sun Priest and the Witch-Woman," a *high and hoarse* voice; a woman may be given a *tight* (tense) or a *high and tight* voice; a mountain lion may be given a *low and gravelly* voice. In other cases voice qualities depend on situations rather than on particular characters: the words "he pulled" may be rendered *with strain*, as if the narrator were trying to hold his breath during great exertion; a character who is starving may speak *weakly;* a sleepy owl may sound as if he were *almost yawning;* a man planning to witch someone may speak with a *rasping* voice.

Italicized notations are also useful when events other than speaking itself play a part in a narrative, as when the performer clears his throat, sighs, breaks into laughter, turns his head to make an aside, or gestures. The two narrators represented here make relatively little use of gestures, mostly limiting themselves to indications (with extended arm and hand) of the position of the sun or the direction in which a story character is traveling. I never worked out an efficient system for correlating these gestures with the narrative texts while in the field (my tape-recorder did not have a counter), so most of them have been lost; the few which remain are indicated by parenthetical notes. In any case, a Zuni gesture is almost never essential to the understanding of the accompanying line, the only real exception in the present collection being this passage from "Coyote and Junco": "Coyote has no teeth here (*points to molars*)."

A Zuni audience usually responds to a narrative with affirmations: in the case of telapnaawe the listeners say "eeso," and in the case of "The Beginning" they say "hacchi" or "eleete," which are more serious and formal than "eeso." Such responses come at the rate of once a minute or more and are usually inserted during a pause; they are most likely to occur after an explanatory sentence, especially if such a sentence is delivered as an aside or is followed by a deliberate pause. Unfortunately it is almost impossible to get a Zuni audience to respond fully in the presence of a tape-recorder. The responses noted in "The Boy and the Deer" have been reconstructed: those which follow the two introductory formulas are standard for all audiences, and the others are based on the restrained "mm" which Walter Sanchez uttered three times while he listened to this story. The "eeso" in "The Girl Who Took Care of the Turkeys" and the audience comment in Part II of "The Beginning" are given exactly as they occured. Audience laughter is frequent on the tape of "Pelt Kid and his Grandmother," but since written notations of this would create the feeling of "canned" laughter I have indicated only the narrator's own laughter.

A narrator's uncontrolled moments, of which the laughter just mentioned is one example, are usually eliminated in written presentations. But they are a natural part of performance, and keeping them in translation helps preserve the "live" quality or unexpectedness of the original story. A narrator may get ahead of himself, for example, and then back up to fill in a missing detail, as Walter Sanchez does in "Pelt Kid and his Grandmother." If I were to eliminate this error in translation I would be doing something an oral performer cannot do, which is to erase something he has already said. Moreover, I would be distorting Walter's personal style, for this "error" is one aspect of his general tendency to great haste and excitement. Other aspects, which I have also preserved, include an occasional stutter, a proclivity for ending lines with connective words, and the production of lines of extreme length (ranging up to twice as long as Andrew Peynetsa's longest). Andrew, by contrast, "tries to bring out his stories not fast, but precisely," as Joseph Peynetsa put it. But even Andrew gets carried away sometimes, as in this passage from "The Boy and the Deer":

> Your belly grew large
> you
> you were to deliver, you had pains in your belly,
>> you were about to give birth to me, you had pains in your belly
> you gathered your clothes
> and you went down to the bank to wash.

The "you" in the second line and the repetition of "you had pains in your belly" might be considered errors, but Andrew is quoting an agitated person at this point: his slips actually enhance the story by making the quotation more realistic.

Even when repeated lines are not accidental they are usually removed from written presentations. But repetition is a common feature of oral discourse, whether formal or informal, in any language, and its elimination in writing is self-conscious and artificial. Moreover, such repetition frequently serves obvious poetic ends. The following passage might seem awkward in a prose format, but with pauses and softnesses restored, the repetitions give it greater force:

At that moment his mother
embraced him
    embraced him.

His uncle got angry
    his uncle got angry.

He beat
his kinswoman
    he beat his kinswoman.

Most of the remaining problems encountered in translating
Zuni narratives are of a more conventional nature than the ones
discussed so far. There are, for example, grammatical problems,
as when an incomplete past action is given the present tense in
Zuni instead of the past; such use of the present would sound
awkward in English narrative, so I have chosen to use the imper-
fect instead (see "Coyote and Junco" for examples: each English
imperfect there corresponds to a Zuni present). One other specifi-
cally grammatical problem worth mentioning involves the occa-
sional shifting of the subject of a Zuni verb from its normal
position before the verb to a sentence-final position: instead of the
normal "Le'holh Nepayatamu ikwekkya," or "That's what
Nepayatamu said," the narrator may say, "Le'holh ikwekkya,
Nepayatamu." "Le'holh ikwekkya" alone would have meant,
"That's what he said," but the narrator, as an afterthought, has
gone on to specify the subject of the verb. Arranging the English
translation in a parallel manner preserves this afterthought qual-
ity: "That's what he said, Nepayatamu."

Zuni narratives contain many words, usages, and phrases
which would be absent in completely neutral everyday speech,
including the formulaic frames which enclose telapnaawe, eso-
teric terms borrowed from ritual language, highly formal greet-
ing exchanges, and archaic interjections. "Son'ahchi," which
opens all telapnaawe, and "Lee——— semkonikya," which closes

them, are declared by the Zunis to be untranslatable, so I have left them as they are. In a sense they are not really "words," just as the frame around a landscape painting is not a part of the enclosed scenery. "Son'ahchi" might be rendered as "Once upon a time," but even aside from the unfortunate fairytale connotations of this English formula, it is not as "abstract" as the Zuni one, in that it does have a decipherable meaning. The Zuni formula which sometimes follows "Son'ahchi," on the other hand, does lend itself to a partial translation: the first word in "Sonti inoo——te" is purely abstract, but the second word means "long ago," a split which is appropriate to the fact that this formula is halfway between the "frame" and the "picture." I have preserved this split by using "Sonti lo——ng ago" in the translations.

The esoteric terms used in Zuni narratives usually refer to matters which might also be referred to (by different terms) in everyday life, rather than to matters which are unique to a ritual context. The ordinary term for a coyote, for example, is "suski," but there is an esoteric substitute, "sani," which I have translated into the less common of the two English terms for this animal, "prairie wolf." The ordinary term for "southward" is "ma'ky'a-yakwin," but a narrator may use "alahho'annankwin," or "toward the coral," instead. Some other esoteric terms are metaphorical: "onanne," for example, which ordinarily means "road," may be used to mean "life," and "shipololo," which ordinarily means "mist," may be used to mean "smoke"; I have retained these metaphors in English rather than translating them into "life" and "smoke."

The greeting exchanges in Zuni narratives are more elaborate than those of everyday life. Ordinarily a person might say "Kesshé," which has the effect of "Hi," and be answered with the same or "Tosh iya," "So you've come." But in a story he may say, on entering a house other than his own, "Hom aatacchu, hom chawe, ko'na'to tewanan aateyaye?" and be answered with, "K'ettsanisshe, ho'naawan cha'le, tosh iya, s'iimu." A straightforward translation of this exchange preserves its highly formal character: "My fathers, my children, how have you been passing the days?" "Happily, our child, so you've come, sit down." When the characters who exchange greetings are of great importance they may go to even greater lengths, as they do in "The Sun Priest and the Witch-Woman" and "The Beginning."

The archaic interjections used in Zuni stories, most notably "Tísshomahhá" and "Hanáhha," are difficult to translate: they have no meanings other than the emotions they are supposed to express, whereas all strong English interjections have reference to sex, bodily functions, or religion. Some English interjections are only covert in such reference or lack it altogether, "My goodness!" or "Wow!" for example, but these lack seriousness, and interjections which are archaic in addition sound even worse, "Gadzooks!" or "Zounds!" for example. In the hope that the contexts of the strong Zuni interjections will make their meanings clear, I have chosen to leave them untranslated. But where archaisms of no great weight are placed in the mouths of ridiculous characters, as in "Pelt Kid and his Grandmother," I have given them English translations which sound old-fashioned: thus Pelt Kid's "A'ana ha'la" becomes "Oh, drat!" and his grandmother's "Atíikya" becomes "Dear me!"

Zuni narratives contain no slang (penaky'amme, literally "non-speech"), but at least one slightly substandard term is used: "okyattsik'i," which Zunis translate as "old lady." In "Coyote and Junco," for example, the Oregon junco, or "silo" (a bird), is referred to as "sil'okyattsik'i"; translating this simply as "Old Lady Junco" preserves the original effect quite well.

The Zuni language offers narrators a rich fund of onomatopoeic words; English is also rich in such words, so there is no great translation problem. Even so I have left some of the original Zuni words as they are, especially where they seem more vivid than their English equivalents; in these cases the context usually makes the meaning clear, as in this line from "The Women and the Man": "Tenén! his body fell dead."

Some Zuni proper names are untranslatable, "Payatamu" (a character) and "He'shokta" (a place) for example, but wherever names are at all translatable I have put them into English, as in the case of "Kempewi Ts'ana," or "Pelt Kid," and "Towayalanne," "Corn Mountain." In order to cut down on the number of difficult Zuni words remaining in the English versions of the stories, I have sometimes translated a name even when its meaning is uncertain; this is the case with "Shoplhuwayal'a," for example, which I have rendered as "Standing Arrows" on the basis of a Zuni folk etymology.

The songs which accompany three of the stories have been left untranslated. In the case of "The Hopis and the Famine," the song is in the Hopi language; since it is unintelligible to the Zuni audience, it seems appropriate that it remain unintelligible to the English-speaking one; moreover, the general meaning of the song is explained by the narrator after he sings it, so that a translation would be redundant. In the case of "Coyote and Junco," the song is composed of vocables which have no meaning; they are not difficult for an English-speaker, so I have left them as they are. The song in "The Girl Who Took Care of the Turkeys" is also composed of nonsense vocables, except that "TOK TOK" is the Zuni rendition of the sound made by a turkey; I have left this song as it is because I prefer "TOK TOK" to "gobble gobble." As for the melodic lines of the three songs, I have treated them in a manner analogous to my handling of the chanted lines rather than using conventional musical notation, in order to emphasize that speaking and singing are on a continuum, with chanting in between.

Beyond interjections, proper names, songs, and the like,

there is something else in Zuni narratives which cannot be "translated" in the ordinary sense, and that is the kind of thing which is not *said* but which takes place in the minds of the narrator and his listeners. This is what Joseph Peynetsa had in mind when he suddenly asked, in the middle of our work on a story, "Do you picture it, or do you just write it down?" Of course part of what the Zunis picture depends on their specific cultural background, and although I have provided some notes to help readers fill in that picture, nothing I could do would make them experience these stories precisely as a Zuni does. But there is no single, "correct" picture of a given story even from one Zuni to another. What makes a narrative work for anyone other than the narrator himself is this very openness, and I think that some of the present narratives are open enough to permit the reader to do some picturing of his own. As Joseph says, "If someone tells a story, you can just imagine it."

NOTES

1   In using "Zuni," rather than the Spanish "Zuñi," I follow the practice, in both spelling and pronunciation, of the English-speaking residents of the Zuni region, including bilingual Zunis; this is the spelling used by the Zuni tribal government. "Zuñi" is a Spanish corruption of the Keresan (a Pueblo Indian language) corruption of the Zuni "Shiwi"; if anything, "Zuñi" resembles the original Zuni word even less than "Zuni" does.

2   For detailed descriptions of Zuni, see especially Matilda Coxe Stevenson, "The Zuni Indians," *Annual Report of the Bureau of American Ethnology*, 23 (1904); Ruth L. Bunzel, "Introduction to Zuni Ceremonialism," *Annual Report of the Bureau of American Ethnology*, 47 (1932), 467–544; and Dorothea C. Leighton and John Adair, *People of the Middle Place* (New Haven: HRAF Press, 1966).

3 For the best description of this ceremony, see Edmund Wilson, *Red, Black, Blond, and Olive* (New York: Oxford University Press, 1956), 3–42.

4 *The Content and Style of an Oral Literature*, Viking Fund Publications in Anthropology, 26 (1959), 7.

5 It is worth noting in this connection that the Zunis have great difficulty in answering when they are asked which character they "identified" with in a given story, even when they have a reasonable understanding of what identification means.

6 Munro S. Edmonson, trans., *The Book of Counsel: The Popol Vuh of the Quiche Maya of Guatemala*, Publications of the Middle American Research Institute of Tulane University, 35 (1971). Dell Hymes has also used semantic structure to break text into lines, as in "Some North Pacific Coast Poems: A Problem in Anthropological Philology," *American Anthropologist*, 67 (1965), 316–341.

7 The principal earlier collections of Zuni narratives, all of them in a prose format, are Frank Hamilton Cushing, *Zuni Folk Tales* (New York: Alfred A. Knopf, 1931); Ruth L. Bunzel, *Zuni Texts*, Publications of the American Ethnological Society, 15 (1933); and Ruth Benedict, *Zuni Mythology*, Columbia University Contributions to Anthropology, 21 (1935). For an extended discussion of the history of the collection and translation of American Indian narratives, see Dennis Tedlock, "On the Translation of Style in Oral Narrative," *Journal of American Folklore*, 84 (1971), 114–133.

8 It is the vagaries of English orthography that make the lines of the Zuni text seem shorter than those of the English translation; the respective syllable counts are reasonably close.

9 Frieda Goldman-Eisler, "Discussion and Further Comments," in *New Directions in the Study of Language*, ed. Eric H. Lenneberg (Cambridge: MIT Press, 1964), 120.

Guide to Reading Aloud

She went out and
went down to Water's End.

·

On she went until
she came to the bank
and washed her clothes.

Pause at least half a second each time a new line begins at the left-hand margin, and at least two seconds for each dot separating lines. Do not pause within lines (even at the end of a sentence) or for indented lines.

Up on the hills
HE SAW A HERD OF DEER.

Use a soft voice for words in small type and a loud one for words in capitals.

The ^{girl} would sit ^{wor}king.

Chant split lines, with an interval of about three half-tones between levels.

O————n he went.

Hold vowels followed by dashes for about two seconds.

KERSPLASHHHHHH

Hold repeated consonants for about two seconds.

aaaaaaAAAAAH

Produce a crescendo when a repeated vowel changes from lower case to capitals.

ta $^{l}a_{a}{}_{a}{}_{a}$

Produce a glissando for ascending or descending vowels.

(gently) Now come with me.

Tones of voice, audience responses, gestures, etc., are indicated by italics.

PRONOUNCING ZUNI WORDS

a, e, i, o, u

Vowels should be given their Continental values.

aa, ee, ii, oo, uu

Double vowels should be held a bit longer than single ones, like the long vowels in Greek.

ch, h, k, l, m, n, p, s, sh, t, w, y

These consonants should be pronounced as in English, except that p and t are unaspirated.

lh

This sounds like English h and l pronounced simultaneously; something like the Ll in Welsh "Lloyd."

,

The glottal stop is like the tt in the Scottish pronunciation of "bottle." When it follows other consonants it is pronounced simultaneously with them.

cch, hh, kk, ll, llh, mm, nn, pp, ss, ssh, tt, ww, yy, "

Double consonants are held a bit longer than single ones, like the double consonants in Italian.

Stress is always on the first syllable except in words marked with accents.

Note: In the songs, the pauses, loudness, lengthened sounds, glissandi, and the pronunciation of Zuni words are as indicated above. The beat follows the stresses and pauses in the words. The contour of the melody is indicated by the ups and downs of each song line; the reader may determine the exact pitches according to his own ear.

Further Note: The reader should not attempt mechanical accuracy to the point where it interferes with the flow of performance.

THE BOY AND THE DEER

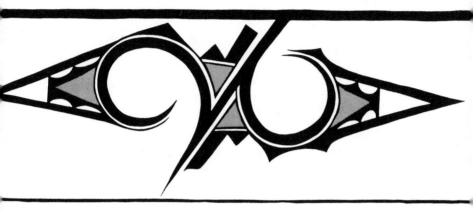

SON'AHCHI.

(audience) Ee————so.

SONTI ^{LO}————NG A _{GO.}

(audience) Ee————so.

THERE WERE ^{VIL}LAGERS AT ^{HE'}SHOKTA

and

up on the Prairie-Dog Hills

the deer

had their home.

                   •

The daughter of a priest

was ^{sit}ting in a ^{room} on the ^{fourth} story ^{down} weaving

^{bas}ket plaques.

She was always sitting and working in there, and the Sun

    came up

every day _{when the} ^{Sun came up}

the ^{girl} would sit ^{working}

at the place where he came in.

It seems the Sun made her pregnant.

When he made her pregnant
though she sat in there without knowing any man
      bel
   her   ly grew large.
She worked o———n for a time
weaving basket-plaques, and
her belly grew large, very very large.
When her time was near
she had a pain in her belly.
Gathering all her clothes
she went out and
went down to Water's End.

          •

On she went until
she came to the bank
went on down to the river, and washed her clothes.

          •

Then

having washed a few things, she had a pain in her belly.

          •

She came out of the river. Having come out she sat down
by a juniper tree and strained her muscles:
the little baby came out.
She dug a hole, put juniper leaves in it
then laid the baby there.
She went back into the water
gathered all her clothes
and carefully washed the blood off herself.

She bundled
her clothes
put them on her back
and returned to her home at He'shokta.

•

And the DEER
who lived on the Prairie-Dog Hills
were going down to DRINK, going down to drink at dusk.
The Sun had almost set when they went down to drink and the
little baby was crying.
"Where is the little baby crying?" they said.
It was two fawns on their way down
with their mother
who heard him.
The crying was coming from the direction of a tree.
They were going into the water

•

and there
they came upon the crying.
Where a juniper tree stood, the child
was crying.

•

The deer
the two fawns and their mother went to him.

•

"Well, why shouldn't we
save him?

Why don't you two hold my nipples
so
so he can nurse?" that's what the mother said to her fawns.

•

The two fawns helped the baby
suck their mother's nipple and get some milk.
Now the little boy

•

was nursed, the little boy was nursed by the deer

o————n until he was full.
Their mother lay down cuddling him the way deer sleep
with her two fawns
together
lying beside her
and they SLEPT WITH THEIR FUR AROUND HIM.
They would nurse him, and so they lived on, lived on.
As he grew
he was without clothing, NAKED.
His elder brother and sister had fur:
they had fur, but he was NAKED and this was not good.

•

The deer
the little boy's mother
spoke to her two fawns: "Tonight
when you sleep, you two will lie on both sides
and he will lie in the middle.
While you're sleeping

I'll go to Kachina Village, for he is without clothing,

    naked, and

this is not good."

•

That's what she said to her children, and
there
at the village of He'shokta

•

were young men
who went out hunting, and the young men who went out
    hunting looked for deer.
When they went hunting they made their kills around the
    Prairie-Dog Hills.
And their mother went to Kachina Village, she went
    o————n until she reached Kachina Village.
It was filled with dancing kachinas.

•

"My fathers, my children, how have you been passing the
    days?" "Happily, our child, so you've come, sit down,"
    they said.
"Wait, stop your dancing, our child has come and must have
    something to say," then the kachinas stopped.
The deer sat down
    the old lady deer sat down.
A kachina priest spoke to her:
"Now speak.
You must've come because you have something to say."

"YES, in TRUTH

I have come because I have something to SAY.

There in the village of He'shokta is a priest's daughter

who abandoned her child.

We found him

we have been raising him.

But he is poor, without clothing, naked, and this

is not good.

So I've come to ask for clothes for him," that's what she said.

"Indeed." "Yes, that's why I've come, to ask for clothes for
     him."

"Well, there is always a way," they said.

Kyaklo

laid out his shirt.

Long Horn put in his kilt and his moccasins.

•

And Huututu put in his buckskin leggings

he laid out his bandoleer.

•

And Pawtiwa laid out his macaw headdress.

•

Also they put in the BELLS he would wear on his legs.

•

Also they laid out

•

strands of turquoise beads

moccasins.

So they laid it all out, hanks of yarn for his wrists and
   ankles
they gathered all his clothing.

When they had gathered it his mother put it on her back:

   "Well, I must GO
but when he has grown larger I will return to ask for clothing
   again."
That's what she said. "Very well indeed."

Now the deer went her way.

When she got back to her children they were all sleeping.

When she got there they were sleeping and she

lay down beside them.

The little boy, waking up

began to nurse, his deer mother nursed him

and he went back to sleep.

   So they spent the night and then
(with pleasure) the little boy was clothed by his mother.
His mother clothed him.

                    •

When he was clothed he was no longer cold.
He went around playing with his elder brother and sister,
   they would run after each other, playing.
They lived on this way until he was grown.
And THEN
they went back up to their old home on the Prairie-Dog Hills.
   Having gone up
they remained there and would come down only to drink, in
   the evening.
There they lived o————n for a long time

until

from the village

his uncle

went out hunting. Going out hunting

he came along

down around

Worm Spring, and from there he went on towards

•

the Prairie-Dog Hills and came up near the edge of a valley
    there.
When he came to the woods on the Prairie-Dog Hills he looked
    down and

THERE IN THE VALLEY was the herd of deer. In the herd
    of deer

there was a little boy going around among them
dressed in white.
He had bells on his legs and he wore a macaw headdress.
He wore a macaw headdress, he was handsome

    surely it was a boy

a male

a person among them.

While he was looking

    the deer mothers spotted him.
When they spotted the young man they ran off.
There the little boy outdistanced the others.

•

"Haa——, who could that be?"
That's what his uncle said.

    "Who

could you be? Perhaps you are a daylight person."

That's what his UNCLE thought and he didn't do
    ANYTHING to the deer.
He returned to his house in the evening.

                              •

It was evening
dinner was ready
        and when they sat down to eat
the young man spoke:
"Today, while I was out hunting
when I reached the top
of the Prairie-Dog Hills, where the woods are, when I reached the top
    THERE in the VALLEY was a HERD OF DEER.
There was a herd of deer

                              •

and with them was a LITTLE BOY:
whose child could it be?
When the deer spotted me they ran off and he outdistanced
        them.
He wore bells on his legs, he wore a macaw headdress, he was
        dressed in white."
That's what the young man was saying
telling his father.
It was one of the boy's OWN ELDERS
his OWN UNCLE had found him. *(audience)* Ee——so.
His uncle had found him.

                              •

Then
he said, "If
the herd is to be chased, then tell your Bow Priest."

That's what the young man said. "Whose child could this be?
PERHAPS WE'LL CATCH HIM."
That's what he was saying.
A girl

a daughter of the priest said

"Well, I'll go ask the Bow Priest."
She got up and went to the Bow Priest's house.
Arriving at the Bow Priest's house

she entered:

"My fathers, my mothers, how have you been passing the
days?" "Happily, our child
so you've come, sit down," they said. "Yes.
Well, I'm
asking you to come.
Father asked that you come, that's what my father said," that's
what she told the Bow Priest.
"Very well, I'll come," he said.
The girl went out and went home

and after a while the Bow Priest came over.
He came to their house
while they were still eating.

•

"My children, how are you
this evening?" "Happy
sit down and eat," he was told.
He sat down and ate with them.
When they were finished eating

"Thank you," he said. "Eat plenty," he was told.
He moved to another seat

•

and after a while

the Bow Priest questioned them:

"NOW, for what reason have you

summoned ME?

Perhaps it is because of a WORD of some importance that
    you have

summoned me. You must make this known to me

so that I may think about it as I pass the days," that's what
    he said.

"YES, in truth

today, this very day

my child here

went out to hunt.

Up on the Prairie-Dog Hills, there

HE SAW A HERD OF DEER.

But a LITTLE BOY WAS AMONG THEM.

Perhaps he is a daylight person.

Who could it be?

He was dressed in white and he wore a macaw headdress.

When the deer ran off he OUTDISTANCED them:

he must be very fast.

That's why my child here said, 'Perhaps

they should be CHASED, the deer should be chased.'

He wants to see him caught, that's what he's thinking.

Because he said this

I summoned you," he said. "Indeed."

"Indeed, well

•

perhaps he's a daylight person, what else can he be?

It is said he was dressed in white, what else can he be?"
That's what they were saying.
"WHEN would you want to do this?" that's what he said.
The young man who had gone out hunting said,

    "Well, in four days

so we can prepare our weapons."
That's what he said.
"So you should tell your people that in FOUR DAYS
    there will be a deer chase."
That's what
he said. "Very well."

          •

(sharply) Because of the little boy the word was given
    out for the deer chase.
The Bow Priest went out and shouted it.
When he shouted the VILLAGERS
heard him.
(slowly) "In four days there will be a deer chase.
A little boy is among the deer, who could it be? With luck
you might CATCH him.
We don't know who it will be.
You will find a child, then," that's what he SAID as
    he shouted.

          •

Then they went to sleep and lived on with anticipation.
Now when it was the THIRD night, the eve of the chase

          •

the deer
spoke to her son
when the deer had gathered:

"My son." "What is it?" he said.

"Tomorrow we'll be chased, the one who found us is your
    uncle.

When he found us he saw you, and that's why

•

we'll be chased.

They'll come out after you:

your uncles.

•

(excited) The uncle who saw you will ride a spotted
    horse, and HE'LL BE THE ONE who

WON'T LET YOU GO, and

your elder brothers, your mothers

no

he won't think of killing them, it'll be you alone

he'll think of, he'll chase.

You won't be the one to get tired, but we'll get tired.

It'll be you alone

WHEN THEY HAVE KILLED US ALL

and you will go on alone.

Your first uncle

will ride a spotted horse and a second uncle will ride
    a white horse.

THESE TWO WILL FOLLOW YOU.

You must pretend you are tired but keep on going

and they will catch you.

But WE

MYSELF, your elder SISTER, your elder BROTHER

ALL OF US

will go with you.

Wherever they take you we will go along with you."

That's what his deer mother told him

that's what she said.

THEN HIS DEER MOTHER TOLD HIM EVERYTHING:
"AND NOW

I will tell you everything.

From here

from this place

where we're living now, we went down to drink. When
we went down to drink

it was one of your ELDERS, one of your OWN ELDERS

your mother who sits in a room on the fourth story
down making basket-plaques:

IT WAS SHE

whom the Sun had made pregnant.

When her time was near

she went down to Water's End to the bank

to wash clothes

and when you were about to come out

she had pains, got out of the water

went to a TREE and there she just DROPPED you.

THAT is your MOTHER.

She's in a room on the fourth story down making
basket-plaques, that's what you'll tell them.

THAT'S WHAT SHE DID TO YOU, SHE JUST
DROPPED YOU.
When we went down to drink
we found you, and because you have grown up
on my milk
and because of the thoughts of your Sun Father, you have
grown fast.
Well, you
have looked at us
at your elder sister and your elder brother
and they have fur. 'Why don't I have fur like them?'
you have asked.
But that is proper, for you are a daylight person.
That's why I went to Kachina Village to get clothes for you
the ones you were wearing.
You began wearing those when you were small
before you were GROWN.
Yesterday I went to get the clothes you're wearing now
the ones you will wear when they chase us. When
you've been caught
you must tell these things to your elders.

•

When they bring you in
when they've caught you and bring you in
you
you will go inside. When you go inside
your grandfather
a priest

will be sitting by the fire. 'My grandfather, how have you
been passing the days?'
'Happily. As old as I am, I could be a grandfather to anyone,
for we have many children,' he will say.
'Yes, but truly you are my real grandfather,' you will say.
When you come to where your grandmother is sitting,
'Grandmother of mine, how have you been passing the
days?' you will say.
'Happily, our child, surely I could be a grandmother
to anyone, for we have the whole village as our
children,' she will say.
Then, with the uncles who brought you in and
with your three aunts, you will shake hands.
'WHERE IS MY MOTHER?' you will say.
'Who is your mother?' they will say. 'She's in a room
on the fourth story down making basket-plaques,
tell her to come in,' you will say.

•

Your youngest aunt will go in to get her.
When she enters:
(sharply) 'There's a little boy who wants you, he says
you are his mother.'
(tight) 'How could that be? I don't know any man, how
could I have an offspring?'
'Yes, but he wants you,' she will say
and she will force her to come out.
THEN THE ONE WE TOLD YOU ABOUT WILL COME
OUT:

you will shake hands with her, call her mother. 'Surely
    we could be mothers to anyone, for we have the
    whole village as our CHILDREN,' she will say to you.
'YES, BUT TRULY YOU ARE MY REAL MOTHER.
There, in a room on the fourth story down
you sit and work.
My Sun Father, where you sit in the light
my Sun Father
made you pregnant.
When you were about to deliver
it was to Water's End
that you went down to wash. You washed at the bank
and when I was about to come out
when it hurt you
you went to a tree and just dropped me there.
You gathered your clothes, put them on your back, and
    returned
to your house.
But my MOTHERS
HERE
found me. When they found me
because it was on their milk
that I grew, and because of the thoughts of my Sun Father
I grew fast.
I had no clothing
so my mother went to Kachina Village to ask for clothing.'
THAT'S WHAT YOU MUST SAY."

•

That's what he was told

that's what his mother told him. "And
tonight
(aside) we'll go up on the Ruin Hills."
That's what the deer mother told her son. "We'll go to the
Ruin Hills
we won't live here anymore.
(sharply) We'll go over there where the land is rough
for TOMORROW they will CHASE us.
Your uncles won't think of US, surely they will think of YOU
ALONE. They have GOOD HORSES," that's what
his mother told him. It was on the night before
that the boy
was told by his deer mother.
The boy became
so unhappy.

They slept through the night
and before dawn the deer
went to the Ruin Hills.

•

They went there and remained, and the VILLAGERS
AWOKE.
It was the day of the chase, as had been announced, and the
people were coming out.
They were coming out, some carrying bows, some on foot and
some on horseback, they kept on this way
o————n they went on
past Stone Chief, along the trees, until they got to the
Prairie-Dog Hills and there were no deer.

Their tracks led straight and they followed them.
Having found the trail they went on until
when they reached the Ruin Hills, there in the valley
beyond the thickets there
was the herd, and the
young man and two of his elder sisters were chasing each other
by the edge of the valley, playing together.

      Playing together
they were spotted.

The deer saw the people.
They fled.

Many were the people who came out after them
now they chased the deer.

Now and again they dropped them, killed them.
Sure enough the boy outdistanced the others, while his
      mother and his elder sister and brother
still followed their child. As they followed him
he was far in the lead, but they followed on, they were
      on the run
and sure enough his uncles weren't thinking about killing
      deer, it was the boy they were after.
And ALL THE PEOPLE WHO HAD COME
      KILLED THE DEER
            killed the deer
                  killed the deer.
Wherever they made their kills they gutted them, put them on
      their backs, and went home.
Two of the uncles

                 •

then

went ahead of the group, and a third uncle

(voice breaking) dropped his elder sister
his elder brother
his mother.
He gutted them there
while the other two uncles went on. As they
    went ON
the boy pretended to be tired. The first uncle pleaded:
    "Tísshomahhá!
STOP," he said, "Let's stop this contest now."
That's what he was saying as
the little boy kept on running.
As he kept on his bells went telele.
O———n, he went on this way
on until

          •

the little boy stopped and his uncle, dismounting
caught him.

          •

Having caught him
(gently) "Now come with me, get up," he said.
His uncle
helped his nephew get up, then his uncle got on the horse.
They went back. They went on
until they came to where his mother and his elder sister and
    brother were lying
and the third uncle was there. The third uncle was there.
"So you've come." "Yes."
The little boy spoke:

    "This is my mother, this is my
elder sister, this is my elder brother.

They will accompany me to my house.

They will accompany me," that's what the boy said.

"Very well."

His uncles put the deer on their horses' backs.

On they went, while the people were coming in
        coming in, and still the uncles didn't arrive, until at nightfall
the little boy was brought in, sitting up on the horse.

It was night and the people, a crowd of people, came out to
        see the boy as he was brought in on the horse through the
        plaza

and his mother and his elder sister and brother

came along also

as he was brought in.

His grandfather came out. When he came out the little boy and
        his uncle dismounted.

His grandfather took the lead with the little boy following,
        and they went up.

When they reached the roof his grandfather

made a corn-meal road

and they entered.

His grandfather entered

with the little boy following

while his

uncles brought in the deer. When everyone was inside

•

the little boy's grandfather spoke: "Sit down," and the little
        boy spoke to his grandfather as he came to where he was
        sitting:

"Grandfather of mine, how have you been passing the days?"
        that's what he said.

"Happily
        our child
surely I could be a grandfather to anyone, for we have the whole

village as our children." "Yes, but you are my real
grandfather," he said.

When he came to where his grandmother was sitting
he said the same thing.

"Yes, but surely I could be a grandmother to anyone, for we
have many children." "Yes, but you are my real
grandmother," he said.

He looked the way

his uncle had described him, he wore a macaw headdress and
his clothes were white.

He had new moccasins, new buckskin leggings.

He wore a bandoleer and a macaw headdress.

He was a stranger.

He shook hands with his uncles and shook hands with his
aunts.

"WHERE IS MY MOTHER?" he said.

.

"She's in a room on the fourth story down weaving basket-
plaques,"
he said.

"Tell her to come out."

Their younger sister went in.

"Hurry and come now:
some little boy has come and says you are his mother."

(tight) "How could that be?
I've never known any man, how could I have an offspring?"
she said.

.

"Yes, but come on, he wants you, he wants you to come
out."

Finally she was forced to come out.

The moment she entered the little boy
went up to his mother.

"Mother of mine, how have you been passing the days?"
"Happily, but surely I could be anyone's
mother, for we have many children," that's what
    his mother said.
That's what she said.

                        •

"YES INDEED
but you are certainly my REAL MOTHER.
YOU GAVE BIRTH TO ME," he said.

                        •

Then, just as his deer mother had told him to do
he told his mother everything:

                        •

"You really are my mother.
In a room on the fourth story down
you sit and work.
As you sit and work
the light comes through your window.
My Sun Father
made you pregnant.
When he made you pregnant you
sat in there and your belly began to grow large.
Your belly grew large
you
you were about to deliver, you had pains in your belly, you

were about to give birth to me, you had pains in your
    belly
you gathered your clothes
and you went down to the bank to wash.
When you got there you
washed your clothes in the river.
When I was about to COME OUT and caused you pain
you got out of the water
you went to a juniper tree.
There I made you strain your muscles
and there you just dropped me.
When you dropped me
you made a little hole and placed me there.
You gathered your clothes
bundled them together
washed all the blood off carefully, and came back here.
When you had gone
my elders here
came down to DRINK
and found me.
They found me

                    •

I cried
and they heard me.
Because of the milk
of my deer mother here
my elder sister and brother here
because of
their milk
I grew.

I had no clothing, I was poor.

My mother here went to Kachina Village to ask for my
  clothing.

•

That's where

she got my clothing.

That's why I'm clothed. Truly, that's why I was among them

that's why one of you

who went out hunting discovered me.

You talked about it and that's why these things happened

  today." *(audience)* Ee————so.

That's what the little boy said.

•

"THAT'S WHAT YOU DID AND YOU ARE MY REAL

  MOTHER," that's what he told his mother. At that moment

    his mother

embraced him

  embraced him.

His uncle got angry

  his uncle got angry.

He beat

his kinswoman

he beat his kinswoman.

That's how it happened.

The boy's deer elders were on the floor.

His grandfather then

spread some covers

on the floor, laid them there, and put strands of turquoise

  beads on them.

After a while they skinned them.

With this done and dinner ready they ate with their son.

·

They slept through the night, and the next day
the little boy spoke: "Grandfather." "What is it?"
"Where is your quiver?" he said. "Well, it must be hanging
    in the other room," he said.

·

He went out, having been given the quiver, and wandered
    around.
He wandered around, he wasn't thinking of killing deer, he
    just wandered around.
In the evening he came home empty-handed.

They lived on

·

and slept through the night.

After the second night he was wandering around again.

The third one came

and on the fourth night, just after sunset, his mother
spoke to him: "I need
the center blades of the yucca plant," she said.
"Which kind of yucca?"
"Well, the large yucca, the center blades"
        that's what his mother said. "Indeed.

Tomorrow I'll try to find it for you," he said.
(aside) She was finishing her basket-plaque and this was for
        the outer part. (audience) Ee⸱——so.
That's what she said.

The next morning, when he had eaten
he put the quiver on and went out.

He went up on Big Mountain and looked around until he
found a large yucca
with very long blades.

•

"Well, this must be the kind you talked about," he said.

It was the center blades she wanted.
He put down his bow and his quiver

got hold of the center blades, and began to pull.
(with strain) He pulled

•

it came loose suddenly
and he pulled it straight into his heart.
There he died.

•

He died
and they waited for him but he didn't come.

•

When the Sun went down
and he still hadn't come, his uncles began to worry.
They looked for him.
They found his tracks, made torches, and followed him
until they found him with the center blades of the yucca in
his heart.

•

Their
nephew

was found and they brought him home.
The next day

•

he was buried.
Now he entered upon the roads
of his elders.
THIS WAS LIVED LONG AGO. LEE————
SEMKONIKYA.

NOTES

Narrated by Andrew Peynetsa on the evening of January 20, 1965, with
Walter Sanchez and myself present; the responses (marked *audience*) are
Walter's. The performance took half an hour.

The village of He'shokta: in the "long ago," this and the villages men-
tioned in the other stories were composed of rectangular, flat-roofed
masonry houses grouped into terraced buildings of several stories,
loosely arranged around a central plaza.

The birth of the boy: describing this in English, Andrew said, "She drops
him like an ewe, by a juniper tree." The mother abandons the boy
because, according to Joseph Peynetsa, "she was supposed to be a priest's
daughter, meaning that she's not supposed to have child out of wedlock;
a priest's family sets an example for the people." Water's End is several
miles from He'shokta; Andrew said, "She went that far so no one would
know what she was doing."

Kachina Village: this lies beneath the surface of a lake and comes to life
only at night; it is the home of all the kachinas, the ancestral gods of the
Zunis. Kachinas are impersonated by the Zunis in masked dances.

Kyaklo: one of the priests of Kachina Village; his face is bordered by a
rainbow and the milky way, his ears are squash-blossoms, rain falls from
his eyes and mouth, and he is unable to walk. His shirt is of white cotton
cloth with an embroidered border.

Long Horn: another kachina priest; he has a long blue horn at the right side of his head, his long left eye extends out onto his left (and only) ear, and he walks with stiff stomping. His kilt is of white cotton cloth with an embroidered border; his moccasins are of a type (ketomaawe) decorated with red, blue, and yellow flaps.

Huututu: deputy to Long Horn; he lacks Long Horn's asymmetry and walks less stiffly. His bandoleer is decorated along its entire length with small conch shells.

Pawtiwa: the chief priest of the kachinas; he has a blue face, blue beak, large furry ears, and his eyes are formed by a black, two-billowed cloud; he is tall and moves in a stately manner. His headdress is a tall bunch of macaw tail-feathers worn upright at the back of the head (macaws were traded from Mexico).

The boy's bells: these are sleigh bells on leather straps (similar bells, made of copper, were traded from Mexico in pre-Columbian times).

"Daylight person": living human beings are "daylight people"; all other beings, including animals, some plants, various natural phenomena, and deceased humans (kachinas), are called "raw people," because they do not depend on cooked food. The boy is partly daylight, since his mother is daylight, and partly raw, since his father is the Sun and since, as Andrew pointed out, "he was the half-son of the deer mother, because she gave him her milk."

The Bow Priest: in charge of hunting, warfare, and public announcements; he shouts announcements from the top of the highest house.

The deer chase: Joseph liked this episode best, "because the boy is fleeing, and yet he knows he'll be brought back by his uncles, where, in truth, he belongs." He added: "The way my own grandfather told this story, when they caught the boy he was so strong they could hardly subdue him." After the chase the surviving deer scatter all over the countryside the way they are now, and, as Andrew put it, "From there on after, there's no chasing deer like that."

The boy enters his house: in the "long ago," houses were entered through a trap-door in the roof; the boy and his grandfather go up an outside ladder to reach the roof and then down a second ladder into the house. Just before they enter the grandfather makes "a corn-meal road" by sprinkling a handful of corn-meal out in front of them, thus treating the boy as an important ritual personage.

"We have the whole village as our children": as a priest, the boy's grandfather prays for rain and fecundity for the entire village, and everyone in the village addresses him and his family as if they were kin; but the boy insists that they are his "real" kin, not just metaphorical kin.

The mother is beaten: according to Andrew, the uncle did this with his riding whip.

The treatment of the slain deer: Joseph commented, "When deer die, they go to Kachina Village. And from there they go to their re-make, transform into another being, maybe a deer. That's in the prayers the Zunis say for deer, and that's why you have to give them corn-meal and put necklaces on them, so that they'll come back to your house once again." He added, smiling, "I suppose the boy didn't eat the deer meat, because he said, 'This is my mother, my sister, my brother.'"

The yucca plant: this was the broadleaf yucca, or Spanish bayonet, with sharp, stiff blades up to a yard long; the boy's mother wanted these blades for the fibers they contain. Joseph commented, "When you find this yucca while sheepherding, it's always tempting to take it out, but it caused a death in a story, so you're afraid to take it out."

The boy's death: asked whether the boy's mother was responsible for this, Joseph said, "No, I wouldn't say that. I think he was really unhappy. He never stayed home: he went out hunting, but he never thought of killing a deer. Probably he was lonesome, and used to being out in the wilds." Andrew said, "Yes, his mother got blamed, because she sent him to get the yucca; he wasn't just going to do that. Her folks said she shouldn't tell him to get it and that his uncles should go and get it. Probably he had it in his mind to kill himself, that's the way I felt when I was telling it. All that time he was with his deer folks, and all that time he had it on his mind. He never did grow up with his family, but with those deer, in the open air, and probably he didn't like it in the house."

"He entered upon the roads of his elders": that is, in Andrew's words, "The boy went back to the deer forever." He was able to do this because death made him a completely "raw" person; he was no longer partly "daylight."

THE HOPIS AND THE FAMINE

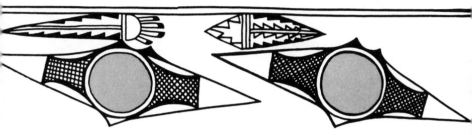

SON'AHCHI.

SONTI ^{LO}——NG A _{GO}.

THERE WERE ^{VIL}LAGERS AT ^{HO}PI

AT LUUHAY

A PRIEST, A YOUNG MAN, HAD HIS FIELDS

AND AT ^{HO}PI THEY WERE GOING TO HAVE

THE ^{FEA}THER-CARRYING DANCE.

They were going to dance
and the dancers were meeting for practice.

They were ^{li}ving this way, meeting for ^{prac}tice
and the young man always went to his fields, that's
    the way he lived.

The day before the dance

                    •

when the young man returned from his fields
his wife
was with her lover.
It seems

                    •

she had a lover.

She went with her lover to his house and there she washed
    and combed his hair
and when the young man came home to his in-laws his wife
    was not there.
Her elders told him she had gone out to the neighbors
to fix their hair.
When the young man
had eaten
    he went over to the neighbors.

His wife

was fixing her lover's hair.

He found out.
He found out.

The young man got angry.
He got angry when he found out and returned to his own
    house.
He took out his bundle of feathers.
And this
was the day before the dance.
The young man took out his bundle of feathers
and went to his fields at Luuhay.
When he got there he started work on his prayer-sticks.
He worked on his prayer-sticks until he finished.
Finishing them, making them good
he painted the sticks with the clay from The Beginning.
When he had finished them, made them good
he went into his field
into the center of his field.

There in the center

•

he planted the sticks.
Famine was to come.
All waters
were to end.

•

He sent in the prayer-sticks
so that
there would be no rain, but
for his own fields there would be enough to plant yearly.
And at Hopi they danced and danced and danced until it was
    finished.
The next year
the people planted
what seeds they had.
They planted until there were no more, and by the fourth
    year
the earth was completely HARD.
The earth was completely hard
and so
the people
dispersed because of hunger.
Some went to Acoma
and some to Laguna
because of hunger.
The young man's
wife, who had a lover
got married to her lover.

THEY LEFT HER TWO SMALL CHILDREN
WITH THEIR OLD GRANDMOTHER AND THEIR OLD
    GRANDFATHER
TO STAY
while they went to Acoma because of hunger.
And the young man was getting along well in his fields.
JUST AS HE HAD WANTED IT
it was a time of famine
there was nothing to eat.

       •

It had been a year since the people left
      it had been a year.

His two children were still small then, they were
on the cradle-board.
After four years

       •

(sighing) there was really
nothing.
The young man thought, "I'll go to my
village and see whether my children
are alive
or perhaps dead.
Who could be alive after all this?" he thought, and the young
    man
left his fields.
      Having left his fields he went on to Hopi.

       •

And the
grandfather and the grandmother

and the sister and her

younger brother

these four

were barely able to live, but still living, and the very old
    Hopis

were all in one kiva, LYING AROUND ALMOST DEAD
    FROM HUNGER.

They were lying around this way

when the young man came.

On their roof, in the sun

together with their grandfather

the two small children

sat there.

(straining to see) When he was far off, "Someone is coming."

That's what the little boy said. "Where is he?" "There he comes."

"Well it must be someone who eats well"

        that's what their grandfather said.

"Indeed."

He came closer.

•

"It looks like our father."

"Where is he now?" "Well, there he comes."

"Yes, that's him."

They were all sitting there this way

when their father came.

Their father

came closer

    and it really was him.

"Yes indeed that's our father.
Perhaps he's living well
and that's why he's coming."
They were sitting
sitting there when he came up.

•

(shyly) "My father, my children, how have you
        been passing the days?"
"Happily, our
child, so you've come." "Yes."
"Where's
their grandmother?"
(weakly) "She's inside
making parched corn for the children
one more time
with the last remaining ear of corn," that's what
their grandfather said. "Indeed.
Let's go inside."
The young man
and his two children and his
father
went down inside to their grandmother
who was making parched corn with THE LAST
        REMAINING EAR OF CORN.
They were going to be hungry.
They were already hungry.

•

When they entered:
"My mother, how have you been passing the days?"

"Happily, my

child, so you've come." "Yes.

(shyly) I've come

to see you

because it's been a long time

since I left you. That bad thing happened to me

so I left you, and it's been a long time so I wanted to see
   my children

and I thought of coming to see you, and you

are barely able to live."

(weakly) "Well, there's nothing left, only this last ear of
   corn

which I'm parching for the children, then we'll probably
   starve," she said.

"That's why I've come.

Is anyone else around?"

"No.

There is no village.

Everyone has left for Acoma because of hunger," that's what she said.

"Indeed."

•

"There might be someone else around:

there might be old people

gathered in the kiva.

Perhaps a few of them are still alive," that's what she said.

•

"VERY WELL, I'LL BE BACK," he said.

The young man then

went back to his fields.

The young man

went into his fields and picked some CORN.

Having picked some CORN

he got together a sack of corn-meal and

ears of sweet corn and

melons and

rolls of paper-bread.

Having gathered these

he went back a second time

to leave them with his small children.

Then they ate.

They were safe now.

The next day

the young man

came again

and spoke to his son. His son had been growing.

"My son," he said. "What is it?"

"I'm going to take you with me."

That's what he said.

His grandfather said, "Very well, you

may go with your father."

The boy went back with his father.

They went on together

until they came to his cornfield.

The boy was amazed.

There was so much in the field

all over the plot

tall corn

melons, watermelons

all of them grown.

⋅

The father took his son into the field

and built a fire to ROAST him some CORN.

When he had roasted some corn the boy ate the corn.

He filled himself. "Are you full?" "Yes."

"Now you'll have plenty to eat," he told him.

Again he picked some corn. Having picked corn

he put some venison with it

put some paper-bread with it.

"Take this back with you.

Leave it and then you can come back here," he said. "All
     right."

The boy carried the load on his back and went to his village.

He was taking it to his grandfather, his grandmother, his
     sister.

When he brought it into the house:

"My father asked me to go back." "You may go."

That's what his grandmother told him, and he went back.

He went along WHILE HIS FATHER

WAS SHELLING SOME CORN FOR HIM.

He put the kernels in a sack.

He said to his son, "NOW

you must go back

you must take these corn kernels with you.

⋅

With this sack of kernels on your back you must go

     o————n until

you reach the village.

You must take these kernels to each house

to each dwelling

to each door.

You must go ALL OVER THE VIL LAGE

leaving kernels in every place. If you are lucky and have

     some kernels left over

then you must take these home.

If nothing is left, then that's the way it will be."

That's what his father told him.

"Indeed." "Yes, that's what you must do.

Just before

you reach the village

you must start singing," he told him.

"When you finish the song

you must give the ik'oku call," he told him.

"Indeed." "Yes."

HIS FATHER SANG FOR HIM. He sang

o————n until, when he finished the song

he gave the ik'oku call.

And he sang and sang and sang and gave the ik'oku call.

"DO YOU KNOW IT NOW?" he said. "Yes

     •

I know it."

But the little boy

did not ask his father what the song SAID.

As he was leaving his father said, "When

when you get near there you should start your song, so your

grandmother and your grandfather

and your elder sister will hear you."

"All right."

AS THE LITTLE BOY WENT ALONG HE CARRIED THE

    SACK OF KERNELS ON HIS BACK.

He carried his kernels until he CAME NEAR THE

    VILLAGE.

When he came near he sang:

LOHO ^{HO-}O-O-O IHI ^{HI-}I-I

HAW,_{'U-U} HAW_{'U}

HA-A-^{A-AAA}A HAW'U-U

HA-A-_{A-}_{A-}_A A HAW'U-U

HAW'U-UHA

WU^{HA-}A-_A_{WU}

WUSHA-_{AKKYEWA}

WU-_{UTTIMA}

HU_{WINI}^{WA-}_{A-A-A}

U^{LEWA} ANI_{TI-I}

WUT_{TIYAMA ANI}_{TI-} I

YU-_U YE_{SHE} KI^{WE}_E^E EE

U-UWI _{U-UWI} _{U-U}^{WI}_{HU}

HU-_U ^{LI}_I_I_I

WHEN HE FINISHED HE GAVE THE IK'OKU CALL.
WHEN HE GAVE THE IK'OKU CALL
HIS
grandfather and his grandmother
(frowning) heard him.

·

THEY WERE NOT HAPPY.
AND THE SECOND TIME HE SANG, HE WAS
    SINGING VERY NEAR.
IN THE SONG HIS GRANDMOTHER WAS WUTTIMA
HIS GRANDFATHER WAS SHAKKYEWA
AND THE LITTLE BOY WAS HUWINIWA:
HE WAS CALLING HIS OWN NAME.
HE WAS TELLING HOW THE FAMINE HAD STARTED
    IN THE SONG.
When he sang this
his elders became unhappy.

The third time he sang it
THERE AT THE KIVA
THE OLD HOPIS
WERE LYING AROUND ALMOST DEAD
WHEN THEY HEARD IT.
There was one
who was listening.
"A^{HA}A$_A$."
"What is it?"
"Someone is saying something."
And soon he ENTERED THE VILLAGE and sang.
He sang
and when he sang the Hopis listened to him.
WHEN HE FINISHED SINGING he gave the ik'oku call.
"AHA^{HA}A$_A$
SO THAT'S WHY WE'RE ALMOST DEAD.
BECAUSE OF THAT PERSON
we're almost dead.
TÍSSHOMAHHÁ.
Our children don't know any better.
So that's why
(sighing) there's a famine.
For it is said
that when the wife of a priest is taken
there will be a famine
there will be an earthquake:
SO IT IS SAID and
THAT'S WHY WE'RE ABOUT TO DIE."

That's what the old Hopis were saying
LYING AROUND THINKING, lying around while the
little boy went from house to house
giving out corn kernels. He went on and on a————ll over
the village
going around until
when he got home
he had a few left over.

He entered. When he entered, "My
grandmother, my grandfather, my
elder sister, how have you
passed the day?" "Happily, our son, so you've come home
now." *(seriously)* "Yes, I've come home
and I've done what my father told me to do
and these
I will take
inside there
where the corn used to be stored.
Father said
these will multiply themselves magically.
When we don't have enough parched corn, when we aren't
full
you
must go inside
where the corn is
and bring out AS MUCH AS YOU WISH
for there will always be enough.
That's what
my father told me
that's what he said."

"Indeed."
"Yes indeed."

•

And that's what
he told his grandmother, his grandfather, and his
    elder sister. "Indeed.
THIS IS THE WAY IT WILL BE, but now I must
    go back again," that's what he said.
"Very well, you may go back."
"Do you have enough food now?" the boy said. "Well
well, we have enough food now.
You might be given further instructions."
Again the boy went back to his father.

•

After spending the night, he went back to his father.

"My father, how did you pass the night?" "Happily, so you've
    come."
"Yes." "Have you given out the corn kernels?" "Yes."
"Were they all gone?"
"No, I had a few kernels left and took them home."
"So finally everyone got some."
His father
took some corn and roasted it in the coals for him
he roasted the corn.
The little boy ate the roasted corn
until he was full, and he brought him a melon which he also
    ate and
he set out a roll of paper-bread and some venison
    which he also ate, until he was full.

"Are you full?" "Yes."

When he had cleared away the meal:

•

"TOMORROW

I will work on some prayer-sticks," that's what the young man
    said. "Indeed."

"Yes, I will work on some prayer-sticks tomorrow.

How IS it?

Does your grandfather still have some food left?"

•

"Yes, they have some food left:

that's what they told me."

That's what he said to his father.

"You must take some more corn to them

and then you can come back here to stay with me.

Then

you will stay here with me about four nights

and then you may go back," that's what his father told him.

"Indeed." "Yes, that's what we must tell your elders

    so they won't wait for you," he said.

"All right." So his father gathered some CORN

a sack of corn-meal

some corn, some rolls of paper-bread, some venison

some melons.

When all these had been gathered they took them there

to his house.

Now they had enough food

so the boy

and his father told them.

"Very well, we won't expect you until then."

When this had been said THEY LEFT, AND THE NEXT
DAY

he worked on his sticks, the PRIEST.

He made the sticks.

It was about noon when he finished the sticks.

He painted them with the clay from The Beginning,
and when he had finished

the young man spoke:

"Son." "What is it?"

"You must sit at the door," he said.

"All right."

"And I will go to the center of the field

with the prayer-sticks

and give the prayer-sticks to the Uwanammi."

There

in his shelter there

at the end of the field

he brought out

his sacred bundle.

Having brought it out

●

HE SANG A STRING OF PRIESTLY SONGS.

He sang priestly songs.

He kept on singing, singing these until he had sung them
four times.

He told his son, "Look outside and see if anyone
is coming up," but

he did not say, "See if the clouds are coming up."

The boy went out
and looked all around.

    (aside) "No one is coming up."
And he sang and sang
and the second time he sang, he asked him
to look again.
The fourth time he sang
when he had sung the first part
he told his son, "Look outside and see if anyone
     is coming up."
(aside) It THUNDERED.
It thundered.

"Are they coming up?" "Well now
the clouds are getting very dark." "They're the ones I'm
     talking about," he said.
"THE CLOUDS ARE SWELLING," the boy said.
He sat down again and sang, and the rain came
aaaaaaAAAAAAH
ALL OVER HOPI IT WAS REALLY RAINING.

                  •

That's how it happened.
It rain rain rained and
all his fields were full of WATER.
THE OLD HOPI MEN WERE ALMOST DEAD
THEY WERE BARELY ALIVE, alive
when it rained. When the rain passed
the next day
he said to his son, "Son." "What is it?"

"SOME PEOPLE ARE LYING INSIDE THE KIVA
        (aside) ALMOST DEAD.
You must take them this sack of corn-meal
five melons
and this sack of corn-meal.
You must take this sack to them
and feed them. You will break the melons, take out
the flesh and FEED THEM and THEY WILL GET WELL.
They will go to their own homes, bring back corn kernels
parch the corn
FILL THEMSELVES and then go home again," that's what
that's what he told his son, (aside) and that's why
        he was supposed to take these things to them.
He took the food, and when he got there
he went inside.
They were almost dead.
When he entered, "My grandfathers, my fathers,
        how have you been passing the days?"
(weakly) "Happily, our child.
So you've come in," they said. "Yes.
I've come in, I've come in to FEED you.
My father
told me to, that's why I've come.
That's why I'm here." "Tísshomahhá, our child.
(sighing) It's because of your PARENTS
        that we're ALmost DEAD.
It's because of your parents that we're almost DEAD.
Who was singing, was it you?" they said.
"Yes, it was me." "Indeed.

Are you HUWINIWA?" they asked him. "Yes."

"Haa————, so it's your father

who is a priest

for the old ones spoke of this.

So that's why this was done, and that's why

we're about to die."

"You will NOT die.

You must get up," he told them. *(hoarsely)* "Why, we can't

even get up, *(aside)* you must feed us lying down," they

said.

THE LITTLE BOY BROKE A MELON AND TOOK OUT

THE FLESH

AND MIXED THE FLESH

WITH CORN-MEAL TO MAKE DOUGH, AND WENT

AROUND FEEDING THEM, FEEDING THEM UNTIL

when he had used a couple of melons to make dough

they were full. "ARE YOU FULL?" "Yes, we've eaten

but we must get WARM, we'll lie here until we get WARM."

He went out to get some kindling and when he came back in

he built them a fire.

He said, "My fathers, grandfathers of mine

you will get well, get well and WARM YOURSELVES

and you will go to your own houses, and each of you will

bring corn kernels back here

and in this fire

you will parch

your corn kernels.

THEN YOU WILL EAT ALL YOU WANT

and go back again to your own houses."

"Indeed.

How could it be? We don't have anything, that's why

we're almost dead," they said.

"IN YOUR HOU~SES~

there ~is COR~N.

Because of the thoughts of my PARENT your houses have

HEARTS again.

There are stacks of corn and you need no longer be hungry,

and you must bring some kernels here:

THEN you will eat until you are FULL.

You will be safe, you will not die," that's what the little

boy said.

"Tísshomahhá, our child

is this true?" "YES IT'S TRUE, I'm not lying.

That's why I've come, but now I must go back. May you have

a good night."

"By all means may it be the same with you."

The little boy went out

AND FINALLY THEY ALL GOT UP AND WARMED

THEMSELVES UNTIL THEY WERE ALL WARM.

(with pleasure) THEY BROKE A MELON AND ATE,

AND THE SECOND TIME THEY BROKE A MELON

THEY WERE ALL FULL.

THEY WALKED AROUND.

They could do that now.

They talked about what they'd been told:

"HA'^{AA} MAMA,

      IT MUST BE TRUE."

And having talked, they went to their own houses.

Just as he had told them, there was plenty of CORN,

      stacked where the corn had been stored before.

There was corn of every kind.

When they had eaten they went back to their houses again

and the little boy went on back

to his father, and arrived there.

                                    •

The marks where the water had run were all around, and

far away there at

Acoma

the mother of the two children

said to her new husband, "Why don't you go to our

children's land. Perhaps

our children are dead.

Perhaps our elders are dead

for we came here a long time ago."

That's what

his wife told him. "Yes, I should go."

And then the young man set out from Acoma.

He arrived.

HE RAN ALL THE WAY AND SPENT FOUR NIGHTS
      BEFORE

HE ARRIVED AT HOPI. It was about noon when he came

and again they were up on their roof:

all of them were sitting there.

•

The young man was coming.

(straining to see) "Someone is coming," they said. "There he
    comes, running. Well, whoever it is
must eat well to move that way."

When he got closer they said

"Well, we know who it is. It's our mother's husband."

That's what the two children said. "Indeed."

"Let no one speak to him," they said.

His elder sister went in

and the little boy went in. Having gone in, they spoke to their
    grandmother:

"Our mother's

husband is coming.

When he gets here and comes inside

don't speak to him, for it's his fault

that we almost died of hunger.

Our mother didn't know what was right.

You mustn't speak to him, and we'll see what he does."

They were inside, and only their grandfather was sitting
    outside.

And soon their mother's husband climbed up.

When he climbed up

•

he came

to where their grandfather was sitting.

(with overdone friendliness) "Father of mine, how have you
    been passing the days?"

He didn't answer him at all.

•

He climbed down
and entered.
The two children were with their grandmother
and she was parching corn for them.
When he entered:

"My children, my mother, how have you been passing the
    days?"

No one spoke to him.

•

He spoke to them repeatedly.
The young man went out and
went among the houses.

•

He went around the village
and the smoke was coming out wherever the old people were.
He went all around before
he went back to his Acoma.

They lived on until the boy
went back to his father
and while he was there
he was told the ways of a priest, they lived this way
o————n until the next year
and his mother's new husband, who had come visiting
had told the Hopis at Acoma about the good land
    and the marks all around where the water had run
and then
they were talking about going back to Hopi.

    And the boy had his own
cornfield.

He had a big cornfield.
And one by one they were coming back, and the mother
had made shirts for her children, pants for them:
she had made everything for them to wear.
And they left Acoma and went o————n spending several
    nights, and on the fifth day
THE HOPI PEOPLE CAME BACK TO HOPI.
The mother and her new husband went there
to clothe their children, but no one spoke to them.
They went out and went to their own house
the house of the husband.
O————N ONE BY ONE ALL THE HOPIS WHO HAD
    LEFT BECAUSE OF HUNGER WERE
    COMING BACK, COMING BACK.
They went into their houses
and the storeroom doors would not open
there was so much corn.

          •

The old Hopis
were the ones who
told what had happened, the old ones told it and the others
    told one another.
They told one another

          •

about that person
about the priest's
wife

who didn't know what was right and who almost caused them
    to die, the old Hopis told the others.

And the priest lived on
until he told his son

"Now, my SON, this is the way you will live."
Having said this, he sang the priestly songs, he untied
everything for him.
When he brought his elder sister, he told both of them about
PRAYERS:
he untied these for them.
How to WORK WONDERS:
how to cause great floods and STOP them
how to do EVERYTHING, to cause FAMINES:
he untied everything for them.
And they understood clearly.
The corn grew old.
When the corn grew old
their father said to them, "My children." "What is it?"
"You must go back to your own house.
You will tell your grandfather to summon the Bow Priest.
He will announce that the people will come
here to my fields and haul corn to your house four times.
All the people will come and they will haul it
to your house four times
and they will take whatever is left in the field
for THEIR OWN.
That will be theirs.
When you

•

go back
you will live this way.

Now you have TAKEN MY PLACE.
You will think of all the prayers I have lived by
of the sacred bundle, that's the way you will live.
The wonders, the rituals
whatever I have known
you will live by
and in the future
we do not know what will happen
to you
and I will return to my village
I will return to my home
and there perhaps
I will find another wife. I will find another wife and
you two will replace me
for you are young, and you must do this.
When you go back you must tell the Bow Priest
that there will be a corn harvest on the fourth day."
THAT'S WHAT HE TOLD THEM.
Then, taking their sacred bundle with them
and their paint, they returned to their house.
When they got there they told their grandfather
their grandmother
of all the things their father had told them, of how
    they were now
both
priests

•

and of the things their father had untied for them.
"We must summon the Bow Priest."

Their grandfather summoned the Bow Priest.
The Bow Priest came.
Then the two children told him, "Now
we have become persons of value
and four days from now
there will be a corn harvest at Luuhay.
You will haul it for us four times
including the melons, four times, then you will
bring in
what is yours."
That's what they asked.
"Very well."
The Bow Priest went out and shouted his announcement.

On the fourth day

•

they went out to gather the corn.
When they arrived there was lots of tall corn.
Just as they had been told, they hauled it four times
and then they hauled their own.
That's the way it was lived there.
That's why the Hopis knew how to WORK WONDERS:
how to THROW one another off the CLIFFS
how to ROAST one another
how to cause FAMINES, how to cause great FLOODS and
    STOP them.
That's how these things were untied.
That's how they came to be such knowledgeable people. This
    was lived long ago. LEE————
SEMKONIKYA.

NOTES

Narrated by Andrew Peynetsa, later in the same evening on which he did "The Boy and the Deer." He said that "The Hopis and the Famine" was borrowed by the Zunis from the Hopis and that the song is in the Hopi language, but most of the details of the story fit the Zuni way of life as well as they do the Hopi. The performance took thirty-five minutes.

Feather-Carrying Dance: a social dance, no longer performed at Zuni.

Hair-washing: this is done on the eve of almost any major ceremonial occasion.

Prayer-sticks: these consist of series of feathers tied to willow sticks; the sticks are painted with "the clay from The Beginning," which was brought out of the underworld by the Zuni priests at "The Beginning." Prayer-sticks are "planted" in the ground as offerings to the raw people.

The famine: in causing this, the priest uses his normally benevolent powers to do the people harm. Priests are regarded with suspicion, for, as Joseph Peynetsa puts it, "They get to a place where they know too many prayers, and they say, 'Let me try this, maybe it'll work.'"

The grandparents: these were the maternal grandparents of the two children; when the priest calls the grandfather "father," he means "father-in-law."

Cradle-board: a board to which a swaddled infant is snugly laced with thongs.

Kiva: a rectangular ceremonial chamber, sometimes partially underground, entered through the roof by a ladder.

Foodstuffs: "sweet corn" is the familiar yellow corn. "Parched corn" is usually made from black corn; it resembles popcorn but the kernels are only cracked, not burst. "Paper-bread" is usually made from blue corn; the watery dough is spread on a stone griddle, and the resulting "bread" is in sheets thin enough to be translucent.

The ik'oku call: a tight, high-pitched whine, most commonly heard from some of the kachinas.

The Uwanammi: rain-bringing raw people who live on the shores of the four oceans.

Sacred bundle: one of the principal sources of a priest's power, brought from the underworld at The Beginning. Laymen are not supposed to know exactly what these bundles consist of.

"The marks where the water had run": small eroded channels and alluvial deposits of sand, clay, or leaves and twigs.

The children become "persons of value": this refers to their possession of powerful knowledge rather than to material wealth. The boy becomes the priest proper, while his sister becomes the female assistant which some priesthoods have.

The harvest: in former times, the villagers took care of a priest's fields.

"How to throw one another off the cliffs": according to Andrew, in one of the religious societies at Hopi, "When someone was initiated, he was thrown down to try him out." "How to roast one another" also refers to an initiation trial.

THE GIRL WHO TOOK
CARE OF THE TURKEYS

Son'ahchi.

(audience) Ee————so.

There were villagers at the Middle Place

•

and

a girl

had her home

there

at Wind Place

where she kept a flock of turkeys.

At the Middle Place they were having a Yaaya Dance.

They were having a Yaaya Dance, and

during the first day

this girl

wasn't

drawn to the dance.

She stayed

with her turkeys

taking care of them.

That's the way

she lived:

it seems

she didn't go to the dance on the FIRST day, that day

she fed her turkeys, that's the way

they lived

and so

the dance went on

and she could hear the drum.

When she spoke to her turkeys about this, they said

"If you went

it wouldn't turn out well: who would take care of us?"

that's what her turkeys told her.

She listened to them and they slept through the night.

Then it was the second day

of the dance

and night came.

That night

with the Yaaya Dance half over

she spoke to her big tom turkey:

•

"My father-child, if they're going to do it again tomorrow

why can't I go?" she said. "Well

if you went, it wouldn't turn out well."

That's what he told her. "Well then

I mustn't go."

That's what the girl said, and they slept through the night.

They slept through the night, and the next day

was a nice warm day, and

again she heard the drum over there.

Then she
went around feeding her turkeys, and
when it was the middle of the day, she asked again,
    right at noon.
(tight) "If you
went, it wouldn't turn out well.
There's no point in going:
let the dance be, you don't need to go, and our
lives depend on your thoughtfulness," that's what
    the turkeys told her.
"Well then, that's the way it will be," she said, and
she listened to them.
But around sunset the drum could be heard,
    and she was getting more anxious to go.
She went up on her roof and
        she could see the crowd of people.
It was the third day of the dance.

That night she asked the same one she'd asked before
and he told her, "Well, if you
must go

                        •

then you must dress well.
YOU
must go around
just four times:
you must THINK OF US," that's what he told her.
"You must think of us, for if
you stay all afternoon, until sunset
then it won't turn out well for you," he told her. "Well

well, I'll certainly do as you say: why should I stay there
for a long time?
They get started early and I'll
do as you say," that's what she told her
her
tom turkey.
"Let's get some rest," they said, and they went to sleep,
    but the girl JUST COULDN'T GET TO SLEEP.
So
she got up and built a fire in the fireplace
    then
she made some yucca suds.
She washed her body all over and then went back to bed
    but she couldn't sleep, she was so anxious, she was
EXCITED
about going to the dance, she was so excited. She passed
    the night.
THE NEXT DAY
the sun was shining, and
she went among her turkeys and spread their feed.
When she had fed them she said, "My
fathers, my children, I'm
going
to the Middle Place.
I'm going to the dance," she said. "Be on your way,
    but think of us.
Well
they'll start when you get to those
tall weeds, so

you'll get to the dance in plenty of time," that's what
her children told her. "Then that's the way it will be," she
        said, and she LEFT. *(pained)* It was getting so hot.
It was so hot when
she entered the village.
They noticed her then.
They noticed her when she came up.

She went to where
Rat Place is today, and
when she entered the plaza, the dance directors noticed her.
Then they asked her to dance.
She went down and danced, and she didn't
didn't think about her children.
Finally it was midday, and when midday came she was just
        dancing awa————————y until
it was late, the time when the shadows are very long.
The turkeys said, "Tísshomahhá! our mother, our child
doesn't know what's right."
"Well then, I must GO
and I'll just warn her and come right back
and whether she hears me or not, we'll
LEAVE

                        •

before she gets here," that's what the tom turkey said, and
he flew away.

He flew along until he came to

where they were dancing, and there

                        •

he glided down to the Priest Kiva and perched
on the top crosspiece of the ladder, then he sang:

KYANA_A_A_A_A_AA TOK TOK KYANA_A_A_A_A_AA TOK TOK

YEE-E-E-E HU^{LI}HU^{LI}HU^{LI} TOK TOK TOK TOK
THE ONE WHO WAS DANCING HEARD HIM.
LHA^{PAA————}
HE FLEW BACK to the place
where they were penned, and
the girl ran all the way back.
When she got to the place where they were penned, they
    sang again, they sang and FLEW AWAY, GOING ON
until they came to what is now Turkey Tracks,
    and they glided down there.
When they glided down they stood there and made their
    tracks.
WHEN SHE CAME NEAR they all went away
and she couḷdn't catch up with them.
Long ago, this was lived. That's why there's a place
    called Turkey Tracks. Lee———— semkonikya.

NOTES

Narrated by Walter Sanchez, immediately following Andrew Peynetsa's "The Hopis and the Famine." The response is Andrew's. The performance took seven minutes.

The keeping of turkeys: this is done more for the feathers than for the meat; it started in pre-Columbian times.

Yaaya Dance: in part, a social dance; the dancers form rings around an evergreen tree which is set up in the center of the plaza. The Yaaya was revived in 1969 after a lapse of twenty years.

"My father-child": an abbreviated form of "My father, my child."

"Our lives depend on your thoughtfulness": Joseph Peynetsa said, "Just because there's a dance doesn't relieve you of any responsibilities. If you've had your pleasure, it doesn't mean you have to stay out all day. It's like people who own sheep, maybe they like to see a lot of things that go on, but because they depend on them for their livelihood, they can't just let them stay in the corral and go hungry."

Yucca suds: soap is made from the tuberous root of the yucca plant.

Rat Place: the western entrance to the central plaza of Zuni.

Priest Kiva: the main kiva at Zuni, on the north side of the central plaza. The Priest of the North is supposed to live next to it.

"The top crosspiece of the ladder": not a rung but a stay, high enough to clear a person standing on the top rung.

COYOTE AND JUNCO

SUSKI TAAP SILO

SON'AHCHI.

SONTI I^{NOO—}TE.

•

SHOPLHUWAYAL'AN
SIL'OKYATTSIK KY'AKWAPPA
taachi SUSKI
suski lak a'l iimulhan holh cha'lliye.
Cha'llappa
taachi sil'okyattsik holhi
kyawashey'a.
Teshuk'o
taap k'ushuts'i, holh kyawashey'a.
Il'anna wolunholh lesna
kyawashnan allachelhky'akkya.
Allachelhky'ap
taachi suski
suski' s
lhat allu'ya, yam chal'aawan lhat allu'ya laks

silo kyawashennankwin tecchikya.

SON'AHCHI.

SONTI ^{LO}——$^{NG\ A}_{GO}$

·

AT STANDING ARROWS
OLD LADY JUNCO HAD HER HOME
and COYOTE
Coyote was there at Sitting Rock with his children.
He was with his children

and Old Lady Junco
was winnowing.
Pigweed
and tumbleweed, she was winnowing these.
With her basket

she winnowed these by tossing them in the air.
She was tossing them in the air

    while Coyote
Coyote
was going around hunting, going around hunting for his
    children there
when he came to where Junco was winnowing.

"Kop to LEYE'A?" le'anikwap. "Ma' ho kyawashey'a," le'.

"Kwap to kyawashey'a?" le'. "Ma'

•

teshuk'o taap k'ushuts'i"
    le'holh anikwap.
    "Hayi.
Kop to' ikwe'a?" "Ma' hom luk kyawashnakkya tenanne," le'.

"AMA HOM'AAN TENA'U
akky ho' yam
chawotenna," le'.
Sil'okyattsik s yam
suski an tenakkya:

YUUWA^{HINA}   YUUWA^{HINA}

YUUWA^{HINA}   YUUWA^{HINA}

YU^{HINA}   YU^{HINA}

PHHH PHHH

YU^{HINA}   YU^{HINA}

PHHH PHHH

Le'holh i'.
"EE, HO' SO'AKKYA
ma'so anne, yam ho' cha'aawan tena'unna."
Suski aakya lak wiimayaawan, holh lottikyap
    NIISHAPAK'O AALA'HIPPA
taa yam tenan okky'akkya.

"What are you DOING?" that's what he asked her. "Well,
     I'm winnowing," she said.
"What are you winnowing?" he said. "Well

                              •

pigweed and tumbleweed"
          that's what she told him.
     "Indeed.
What's that you're saying?" "Well, this is
     my winnowing song," she said.
"NOW SING IT FOR ME
so that I
may sing it for my children," he said.
Old Lady Junco
sang for Coyote:

YUUWA^{HINA}   YUUWA^{HINA}

YUUWA^{HINA}   YUUWA^{HINA}

YU^{HINA}   YU^{HINA}

(blowing)   PFFF   PFFF

YU^{HINA}   YU^{HINA}

(blowing)   PFFF   PFFF

That's what she said.
"YES, NOW I
can go, I'll sing it to my children."
Coyote went on to Oak Arroyo, and when he got there
     MOURNING DOVES FLEW UP
and he lost his song.

Ikya ina:

"Hanatte! tom'an tena'u, niishapak hom

tenan okky'anapkya," le'.

Taas an tenne.

Tenan yaanikwatinan taas aakya.

Lak teshoktaawan holhi

taas iskon yeyye an'a kwachukya.

Taas yam tenan okky'akkya.

Taas ha"iky'annan inan

itekkunakkya.

Taas an tenne.

Ha"iky'annana s'anne, taas wiimaya holh tecchippa

K'ECCHO AALA'HIP taas yam tenan okky'akkya.

Aawitenaky'annan iyappa
sil'okyattsik leskwikkya, "Aa lak to' iyappa
kwa'so tenaashukwa," le'kwanas.

A'ky'amon teshuna.

A'ky'amon awana, yam
sil'ucchun ullunan, an sil a'unan kyala"u.

"Shemak yamante ko'le'ona."

Silo yam ky'akwen kwatokya.

Suskis aawitenaky'annan iya.

Inan:

"Hanatte! tom'aan tena'u, taas an tenan okky'anakkya, iya,"
le'anikwappa.

Kwa' silo peyena'ma.

He went back:

(muttering) "Quick! sing for me, some mourning doves made
me

lose my song," he said.

Again she sang for him.

He learned the song and went on.

He went through a field there

and broke through a gopher hole.

Again he lost his song.

Again, he came for the third time

to ask for it.

Again she sang for him.

He went on for the third time, and when he came to Oak
Arroyo

BLACKBIRDS FLEW UP and again he lost his song.

He was coming for the fourth time

when Old Lady Junco said to herself, *(tight)* "Oh here you come

but I won't sing," that's what she said.

She looked for a round rock.

When she found a round rock, she

dressed it with her Junco shirt, she put her basket of seeds
with the Junco rock.

(tight) "As for you, go right ahead and ask."

Junco went inside her house.

Coyote was coming for the fourth time.

When he came:

"Quick! sing it for me, I lost the song again, come on,"
that's what he told her.

Junco said nothing.

"Hanatte!" le'anikwap, kwa' penamkya.

"TOOPA," le'.

"Aawitenaky'annan ho'
penap, kwa'hom'an to' tena'ma, tom ho' uttenna,"
le'anikwappa.

•

"Kwiliky'annan, KWIILI," le'.

"Hanat tom'aan tena'u," le'.

Kwa' tena'ma. "HAA"I. ALHNAT ho' penuwa," le'.

•

Suskis, "HANAT TENA'U," le'anikwappa.

Kwa' tena'ma.

Sil'ucchun suski a"u.

Sil uttep, KWAAM, a'ky'amon s'olh uttekya.

Liilhno luky'anna ko' yo'nashky'an, akkyaluk
yo'na yalhakwin.

"Luhappa tenhish tom ho' leyan." "AY! AY!" le'kwana.

SANI YAM CHA'LIKWIN TECCHIP, kyaakyamash ko'an
chawe yashekkya tekkwin tecchikya.

Le'n inoote teyatikko'akkya, kwa' suski liilhno
aawo'nawamme. LEE————SEMKONIKYA.

"Quick!" that's what he told her, but she didn't speak.

"ONE," he said.

"The fourth time I

speak, if you haven't sung, I'll bite you," that's what

he told her.

•

"Second time, TWO," he said.

"Quick sing for me," he said.

She didn't sing. "THREE. I'll count ONCE MORE," he said.

•

Coyote said, "QUICK SING," that's what he told her.

She didn't sing.

Junco had left her shirt for Coyote.

He bit the Junco, CRUNCH, he bit the round rock.

Right here *(points to molars)* he knocked out the teeth, the

rows of teeth in back.

(tight) "So now I've really done it to you." "AY! AY!"

that's what he said.

THE PRAIRIE WOLF WENT BACK TO HIS CHILDREN,

and by the time he got back there his children were dead.

Because this was lived long ago, Coyote has no teeth here

(points to molars). LEE————SEMKONIKYA. *(laughs)*

NOTES

Narrated by Andrew Peynetsa, immediately after Walter Sanchez did "The Girl Who Took Care of the Turkeys." The performance took four minutes; Andrew learned this story from a man who had a reputation for telling only very short stories.

Coyote: Joseph Peynetsa commented, "These Coyote stories make it sound like he's an outcast and nobody thinks too much of him. So he's the eater of any kind of food, like bugs, roots, berries."

Blackbirds: these are Brewer's blackbirds.

Junco shirt: Old Lady Junco is an Oregon junco, and her "shirt" is the hood-like area of dark gray or black that covers the head, neck, and part of the breast of this species.

Prairie wolf: at this point Andrew uses "sani," an esoteric term for coyote, rather than "suski," the ordinary term; therefore I have used the less common of the two English terms for this animal.

The ending: asked whether this story teaches a lesson, Joseph said, "It just teaches how the coyote is being very foolish. It doesn't teach anything like a human being might do."

THE WOMEN AND THE MAN

SON'ahchi.

Sonti LO———NG AGO.

THERE WERE ^{VIL}LAGERS AT THE ^{MID}DLE PLACE

          •

at KYAKIIMA
the K'UUCHININA PEOPLE had their home
and
at SHUUN HILL
the PAYATAMU
had their home.
At Shuun Hill the eldest of the Payatamu brothers
went out every day
to bring out the Sun.
He started out from Shuun Hill
went on to Kyakiima, and then

          •

at Mats'aakya
at the Rock
of the Sun
he brought his father out, that's the way
they were living, and he went every day

and the K'UUCHININA PEOPLE:
those women were the only people living there
at Kyakiima.
They had been killing wood gatherers.
They were making basket-plaques
living this way
when the eldest of the K'uuchinina sisters spoke:
"Tomorrow morning
I'll go out and wait for the one who always comes by here."
That's what she told her younger sister
told all her younger sisters.

"It's up to you," they told her.

•

And at Shuun Hill, Payatamu started on his way. Payatamu
    started on his way
to bring out his Sun Father, and as he went along
there at Kyakiima
where a rock stood
the telele of his bells could be heard, well, she
    could hear him coming.
When she heard him, she made a bundle with her white
    blanket
putting in her SPEARHEAD
putting in her abalone shell.

•

She put the bundle on her back
and went down to wait for the young man.
She waited near the big rock at Kyakiima
where the young man always came past.

She waited there, and a short time later
the young man came.
When he came

    "Where are you going?" she asked him. "I'm
    going to bring out my Sun Father."

                  •

(high and tight) "He's going to come out ANYWAY.
Why don't we go to my field?" she told him.
"Well, I won't go.
I didn't come just to go anywhere, but to bring out my Sun
    Father."
That's what he said. "Indeed.

                  •

But he's going to come up ANYWAY
just the way he's BEEN coming up," that's what
    she said. "No, it's because of me that he comes up."
That's what he told her, and they kept on arguing this way
    until
after a time, the young man said:
"Well then
if that's the way you feel
I won't go."
That's what the young man said, the girl got the better of
    him.

                  •

"We'll go over there where our field is"
she said, then she took the young man to the field, and the
    SUN HAD NOW COME UP, HE HAD COME UP

and was high now, while the woman took the young man to her

    fields, there at

Hanging Mealbag, where they had their fields.

•

That's where he was led, the girl

led the young man there.

They had their cornfield there

    their cornfield.

They had a shelter there.

The Sun went HIGHER AND HIGHER

until it was about noon.

    It was about noon

when they came to the shelter, and the girl spoke:

    "NOW

THIS DAY

we'll play hide-and-seek.

Whoever is found

must be KILLED," that's what the girl told the young man.

    "Indeed."

"Yes, so you go ahead," she said. "Indeed?

Why should I go first?

You're the one who wanted this, you should go first.

You should be first:

since you're the one who wanted this, I won't go," that's what

    the young man said.

"Very well indeed."

•

The girl then

entered her field.

Entering her field

she came to the middle and then passed one cornstalk,
    she went past the cornstalks:
a second, a third, and when she had passed a fourth one
she fastened herself to a cornstalk and became
AN EAR OF CORN.
When she had fastened herself on

    "NOW," she said.

                              •

The young man
entered the field
and went on, went on until
he came near the end of her footprints.
He passed a cornstalk, the first cornstalk, then went
    on past the fourth cornstalk.
When he got there, the footprints ended.
There were no more footprints.

He went ALL OVER the field and couldn't find her.
He came back and said

    "Oh no
SHOW YOURSELF, for I can't find you." "Aa—pity on you
you haven't been very smart, here I am, FASTENED ON,"
    she said.
She came out of the EAR OF CORN.
The girl came out.

                              •

When they got back to the shelter she said, "Now
    it's your turn, so GO," she said.

(weakly) "Well, I'll
try."
That's what the young man said.

•

The young man entered the field
and did what the girl had done, going past the
    CORNSTALKS, on past the FOURTH cornstalk
but he didn't turn into anything.

•

He stood facing south
and it was already noon
    his father was right at the middle.
"Tísshomahhá! my son
    surely you'll
you'll be KILLED now."
That's what he said, and THE YOUNG MAN STEPPED
    FORWARD, TOOK OUT HIS CORN-MEAL, and
    sprinkled it
toward his father. The corn-meal made a road and he
    followed it up. When he got there to his father,
    he said, "My father, how
have you been?" "Happy, my CHILD.
Tísshomahhá!

•

There will be a lot of TROUBLE now, she will SURELY
    find you and KILL you, just as she SAID.
Even so, sit behind my back," that's what he told his son.

Payatamu

now sat with the Sun, sat behind his back.

"NOW."

Then the girl came out of the shelter. She followed the

young man's footprints where he had passed among the cornstalks

she went on

until she came to where he had stood.

(nasal) "Haa——, so you're trying to find safety."

She unfolded her abalone shell.

When she unfolded her abalone shell

•

she took milk from her own breast

from her own breast

she took milk

and filled the shell with it.

The Sun

was reflected in it. The Sun was reflected in it

and she saw Payatamu's macaw headdress sticking out from

behind the Sun.

(almost laughing) "Haa——, even though you tried to find a

safe place.

Hurry on down, for I've found you," she told him.

He came out.

"Well

that's all.

Because of this we'll be harming a————ll the villages:

I must go in AT ONCE

for I've been coming up because of you.

SHE'S GOING TO KILL YOU, surely she's not just talking,
    she'll kill you," that's what the Sun told his son.
"Now you must go back down

and I will go right in," he told his son.
"I'm going now, and may you pass a happy evening." "May it be
    the same with you," he said.
THE YOUNG MAN CAME DOWN.

                    •

He came down
and these
were the people who'd been killing
the wood gatherers
until now:
that's what they'd been doing.

                    •

THE YOUNG MAN CAME ON DOWN until
he came to where the girl was standing.
She led him along until they came to the shelter.

She unfolded her white blanket
and there was a large spearhead inside. It was WRAPPED.
She unwrapped it and got ahold of his forehead.

"Now, look at your Sun Father for the last time," she said.

                    •

She made the young man look up and she
cut through his throat.
Tenén! his body fell dead.
She held his head while the blood ran, ts'ok'ok'oo——until
    all the blood had drained out
then she set it down

and now she went looking for a place to BURY him.

She went through her field

until she came to its end, where water had run through and
left a deposit of juniper leaves.

There she dug a hole. When the girl had dug a hole

she carried the young man's body there and buried him.

•

She returned to her shelter

and when she picked up his head the blood wasn't dripping.

She wrapped it in her white blanket and, putting it on her
back

the girl went home.

She carried the head, Payatamu's head

going on

until

she reached the house where she lived with her younger sisters.

•

"SO YOU'VE COME NOW," they said. "Yes, I've come
now. JUST AS I INTENDED

I've killed him.

Because of him

we'll be able to continue working.

Each morning he'll be of great value to us," that's
what the girl said.

•

They got together and started working on their
basket-plaques, and they

put the young man's head in a water jar.

•

During the day his headdress would quiver,

      o————n until, in the evening

it would become still:

this was a SIGN for them.

Then they slept through the night.

•

The elder brother Payatamu hadn't come home, and

    FOUR DAYS HAD PASSED.

When four days had passed

•

the Payatamu

men said

"Our elder brother hasn't come home and the days

    have gone by.

Our Sun Father hasn't come up.

What should we do about this?"

•

That's what they said.

Their society chief spoke:

    "Well now

let's try something, even though it might not HELP:

•

we'll ask our grandfathers

to come here.

Perhaps

one of them might find him

for us."

That's what their society chief said.

"Indeed."

"Which one should it be?" he said.

"Well now, our grandfather

who lives in the north, the mountain lion:

let's summon him."

•

Their society chief

summoned the mountain lion.

There in the north he arose, the mountain lion.

•

Coming on and o————n, he arrived at Shuun Hill.
He entered:

"My fathers, my children

how have you been passing the days?" "Happily, our
    grandfather, so you've come now."

"Yes." "Now sit down," they said, and they

set out their turquoise seat for him and he sat down.

•

The society chief sat down facing him.

The mountain lion now questioned them: "NOW, my
    CHILDREN

for what reason have you summoned ME?

You would not summon me for no reason.

Perhaps it is because of a WORD of some importance
    that you have summoned me.

You must make this known to me

so that I may think about it as I pass the days," that's
    what the mountain lion said.

"YES, in TRUTH

our elder brother

who always went to bring out his Sun Father, has been gone
these four days

and hasn't come back.

We don't see our Sun Father anymore.

That's why we summoned YOU.

You must look for him for us," that's what

they told the mountain lion. "Indeed.

Very well INDEED.

I will TRY

but it's different at NIGHT:

we're used to the day," that's what the mountain lion said.

"So that's why you summoned me." "Yes, that's why we
summoned you."

"Very well indeed, I'll GO.

I will try," that's what the mountain lion said, and he left.

When he left the mountain lion went around, went around,

went around

and didn't DISCOVER him. He didn't FIND him. There
wasn't even

a SCENT of him, he couldn't find out ANYTHING.

•

A long time passed
and when the mountain lion failed he came back.

When he came back

he entered:

"My fathers, my children, how

have you been?"

"Happy, our grandfather.

Sit down," they told him. He sat down.

They questioned him.

He hadn't found him.

There was no way to find him.

"During the day

we know more," he said. "Indeed. Very well indeed,
    you must go there

and lie down behind the altar.

When our elder brother has been found

then you may go home and rest," that's what

they told the mountain lion.

He lay down behind the altar, the mountain lion.

And

the society chief said:

   "WELL NOW

who should be summoned next?" he said.

                    •

"Well, perhaps his younger brother

the bear."

                    •

"NOW, the one whose direction is there

toward the evening, the bear:

enter upon our roads," that's what

the society chief said.

After awhile he came, the bear.

The bear came and entered.

"My fathers, my children, how have you been passing
    the days?" "Happily, our child

our grandfather, so you've come." "Yes, I've come."
"Sit down," they said.
A seat was set out and he sat down.

The society chief got up
and sat down facing him.

Then the bear questioned them: "NOW
for what reason have you
summoned ME?
Perhaps it is because of a WORD of some importance that
you have summoned ME.
You would not summon me for no reason," that's what the
bear said. "YES, in TRUTH
our elder brother
who always went to bring out his Sun Father, has been gone
these four days and hasn't come back.
You must look for him for us.
That's why we summoned you"
that's what
the society chief told the bear.

"Indeed.
Very well INDEED.
I will TRY.
During the DAY it's different, we know MORE
but at night
we don't know," that's what he said.

•

"VERY WELL, I'M GOING," he said, and the bear got
up, the bear left and went around.
He went all around, but he couldn't find him.

·

After a long time passed the bear came back and they
   questioned him, and he didn't know.
·

"Then you must go behind the altar
where you will find your elder brother," that's what
      they told him. There behind the altar
was the mountain lion, lying down.
·

The bear lay down there.
   "Now then
think about it: who
should be summoned next?"
·

"OVER THERE
in the coral's direction
the badger
is the one who is wise," that's what they said, and
      the badger was summoned.
And the badger came.
The badger came
·

and entered:
      "My fathers, my children, how have you been
      passing the days?" "Happily, our grandfather, so
      you've come." "Yes," he said.
"Sit down," they told him.
He sat down.

Again the society chief sat down facing him.

Then the badger questioned them: "NOW

my CHILDREN

for what reason have you summoned ME?

Perhaps it is because of a WORD of some importance

that you have summoned me.

You must make this known to me, so that I may think about it

as I pass the days," that's what

the badger said.

"YES, in TRUTH

our elder brother, who always goes to bring out his Sun

Father

has been gone these four days.

Our elder brother hasn't come back.

You must look for him for us, that's why we summoned you"

that's what they told him.

"Indeed.

Well, I will TRY.

But at night one doesn't know, it's during the day

that we are wise," that's what the badger said.

"Well, I'm

going, I will try," he said.

"I'm going, may you

have a good night."

He left.

•

He went around

went around, but he couldn't find him.

He came back, and again they questioned him.

"I didn't find him."

"Very well, then you must go lie down behind the altar."

And the badger went around behind the altar

where his two elder brothers were lying

and he lay down there.

Again they were THINKING.

They were thinking.

"Well now

it should be the one with WINGS," that's what they said.

The eagle was summoned.

The eagle was summoned:

"Now, the one whose direction is the zenith

the one who is our father, the eagle

enter upon our roads."

The eagle CAME DOWN.

He came down until

he arrived there at Shuun Hill.

He entered the Payatamu house.

LHU $^{KW'EE}$ $_{E}$ $_{E}$ $_{ENN}$ he entered.

He sat down on the stone seat.

"My fathers, my children, how have you been passing the
days?"

"Happily, our child, so you've come." "Yes."

The society chief got up and sat facing him, and

he questioned them:

"NOW

my fathers, my CHILDREN

for what reason have you summoned ME?

Perhaps it is because of a WORD of some importance

    that you have summoned me.

You must make this known to me

so that I may think about it as I pass the days," that's what

the eagle said. "YES, in TRUTH

our elder brother

who always went to bring out the Sun, his Sun Father,

    has been gone four days and hasn't come back.

You must go look for him for us, that's why we summoned

    you." "Indeed.

Well, I will TRY.

But it's different at NIGHT:

in the day we know more," that's what the eagle said.

The eagle left.

And the eagle went around, went around looking for him,

    but he couldn't

     couldn't find him.

Again he came.

•

The eagle was told, "Well

you must go now

if he can't be found."

The eagle then left.

Again they thought about it.

The VULTURE was summoned.

The vulture was summoned: that one

is good at SMELLING ROTTEN THINGS, that's why he was

    summoned.

He was the next to come, and he questioned them
and he was told the same thing as before:

that he couldn't be found.

The vulture said

"Well, I will try. During the day we are wise
but at night we don't know," that's what he said.

The vulture went out and went around circling, around and arou————nd

but he couldn't find him, and a long time passed.

.

Again

.

he came. When he came

he entered, tired.

They questioned him. "He can't be found."

"Very well indeed, you must go now.

But these, our fathers, our

grandfathers, must wait until our elder brother has been

found, then they may go home and rest."

The vulture went out and went his way.

.

Again they were THINKING.

.

They were thinking, and

they thought of

the coyote

the one who is the true coyote.

He was the one who was summoned, and he came. He entered and

greeted them, and he sat down.

Then

he questioned them

and was told that their elder brother hadn't returned, and
    that they wanted him back

and so they had summoned him.

    "I will try.

At night

it's hard at night, and in the day also, but I'll
    try," said the coyote. He left

and went around looking. He went looking without
    finding him.

                        •

Again he came.

"Wait now

you must lie down by the door," he was told. THE
    COYOTE LAY DOWN THERE BY THE DOOR, not
    at the altar.

That other coyote

the JUNIPER coyote

was summoned next.

He came, and

he was jittery.

He entered

and greeted them.

He sat down, but he couldn't keep still.

He questioned them:

"Our elder brother, who went to bring out our Sun Father,
    hasn't come back, and these four days have passed.

You must look for him for us, that's why we summoned you,"
    that's what they said. "Indeed.
Well, I will try.
During the day we are wise, but at night we don't know,"
    that's what he said. He went out and

                            •

IT WAS NO USE, but he went around, went around anyway.
Again he came.
Again, "He can't be found."
Again, this one left.
Or rather, he lay down behind the door.
Again they were thinking.
"Well now, someone with wings.
Why not the crow?"
THE CROW WAS SUMMONED, the crow came, the crow
    came and sat down.

                            •

He questioned them, the crow:
"For what reason have you summoned ME? Perhaps it
    is because of a WORD of some importance that
    you have summoned me"
the crow said. "Yes, in truth, our elder brother, who
went to bring out our Sun Father
has been gone these four days, and you must look for
    him for us, that's why we summoned you," they
    told the crow. "Indeed.
I will TRY.
It's different at NIGHT:

during the day we know more," that's what the crow said.
"Well, I'll try," he said, and the crow left.

•

He went around, went around, but he couldn't find him.
Again he came.

He was questioned. "I don't know."

•

"Very well, you must go and rest," that's what they told him.
The crow left.

Again they were THINKING, again

•

they were thinking. "WELL NOW, there is our father
    who lives at the nadir, the MOLE."
That's what their society chief said. The mole was summoned.

•

The mole came.

He came

and entered:

"My fathers, my
children, how have you been passing the days?" "Happily
our grandfather, so you've come." "Yes." "Sit down,"
    he was told, and he sat down.
The society chief again sat down facing him.
Then
the mole questioned them: "NOW
my CHILDREN
for what reason have you summoned ME?
Perhaps it is because of a WORD of some importance
    that you have summoned me.

You would not summon me for no reason," that's what
the mole said. "YES, in TRUTH
our elder brother
who went to bring out our Sun Father, has been gone
    four days and HASN'T COME BACK.
You must look for him for us
that's why we summoned you"
        that's what he said.
"Indeed.
Very well indeed
I will TRY.
These, my elder brothers, have FAILED, so how could I
    SUCCEED?
The way I get around is POOR
it's PITIFUL.
Even so, I will try," that's what the mole told them.
                    •

THE MOLE LEFT.
When he LEFT
                    •

HE FOLLOWED THE SAME ROUTE PAYATAMU HAD
    TAKEN, the mole went on, went o————n until
he came near the K'uuchinina People
near their house, where the rock
was standing.
At the place where they had talked there were still footprints.
There were the footprints:
"Well, this is where you came."

Looking around, he saw their sparks flying out, the
      sparks from the K'uuchinina house.
The mole went up this way. Going up
he climbed the ladder to their doorway

                        •

and LOOKED INSIDE:
they were all around their fire
around their fire, working on their basket-plaques.
PAYATAMU'S HEAD WAS INSIDE A WATER JAR, sitting
      there.
"Haa——, HERE he is.
Why, this
didn't happen very far away
and yet my elder brothers couldn't find him"
the mole said, and AS SOON AS HE HAD SEEN THE
      HEAD
he went down, GOING ON until he came to where
      Payatamu had talked with the girl.
HE FOLLOWED THEIR TRACKS, GOING ON AND
      ON AND O———N until he arrived at the
      CORNFIELD, the mole arrived there.
When he arrived at their cornfield
at the place where Payatamu's head had been cut off
flowers were blooming there
      tenatsali flowers.

                        •

"Haa——, so this is where
he was killed"

he said, and he went on until he came to the place
   where he was buried:
there were a lot of flowers.

"Haa——, he's lying here, not far away, but they couldn't find him.

So THIS is the place."

·

He went straight back
went back

·

and got there after a long time.

He entered:

   "My fathers, my children, how have you been?"
   "Happy, our
grandfather, our child, so you've come now." "Yes."
"Sit down," he was told, and he sat down.
The society chief sat down facing him.
"NOW
our GRANDFATHER
our CHILD
you've gone out to look for our elder brother.
Has he been FOUND NOW?" that's what the society chief
   said.
"He has been FOUND.
He lies not far away, yet my elder brothers here couldn't
   FIND HIM.
Even so, he has been found.
However
how are we going to get his head?"
That's what the mole said.

"Indeed.

Yes indeed."

•

"WELL NOW, THERE IS OUR GRANDFATHER:

let's summon the HAWK, who is very FAST. Perhaps if we
     had him here we could get it."

That's what the mole said. The hawk was summoned.

The hawk came, he came in

LHUUU$_{U_{USU}}$

and lit on a stick on the wall.

•

He lit there

then came down to the seat and sat on it.

"My fathers, my children, how have you been passing the
     days?" "Happily, our child, so you've come now."

"Yes."

•

The society chief went over

where the hawk was sitting.

The hawk questioned him:

"NOW, for what reason have you summoned ME?

You would not summon me for no reason.

Perhaps it is because of a WORD of some importance that
     you have summoned me"

that's what the hawk said.

"YES, in TRUTH

our elder brother

who always went to bring out our Sun Father
has been gone these four days.

          •

We have summoned
our grandfathers here, but they couldn't find him.
The last of our grandfathers to be summoned, the mole
has just found him, but there is no way to get his head, no
      one knows how to do this.
He has said that you are very FAST and should be
      summoned, so we have summoned you."
"Very well indeed, it shall be done," that's what he said.

          •

Again
the mole spoke: "If he's alone it won't work.

          •

YOUR GRANDFATHER, THE OWL, should be
      summoned," that's what he said
the mole said.
When the mole
had told them
      THE SOCIETY CHIEF SUMMONED THE OWL.
The owl was summoned
      and after a time he entered
      the owl entered.
"My fathers, my children, how have you been passing the
days?" "Happily, our child, so you've come now." "Yes."

          •

He sat down, sat down.

As SOON as he sat DOWN he fell ASLEEP.

He was sleeping

when the society chief sat down facing him.

The owl questioned them:

•

(almost yawning) "NOW, my CHILDREN, for what reason
    have you summoned me?

•

•

•

Perhaps it is because of a WORD of some importance
    that you have summoned me, for you would not summon
    me for no reason," that's what he said.

"YES, in TRUTH, our elder brother, who went to bring
    out our Sun Father

has been gone these four days:

that's why we have summoned your elder brothers. He
    has been found now

but there is no way to get his head, and if you were
    included in this your medicine might help:

that's what the mole said, and that's why we summoned you."
    "Indeed.

"VERY WELL INDEED, it shall be DONE."

"Now, let's GET READY."

•

The four Payatamu men then

took PLAIN blankets
two of them.
He led them out, the MOLE.
There were the HAWK and
the OWL
and the Payatamu men.
The mole led them, they went o————n until
they came to where Payatamu had talked to the woman.

•

"This is where they talked, this is where
the two of them talked.

•

Up ahead:
we must go up there, where the K'uuchinina People have
    their home," that's what he said.
That thing

•

that OWL ROOT

•

was given to the mole
and when the root was given to the mole, the mole
went up with the root
and spit the root
on the women.
The women became sleepy, they became sleepy now.
They said, *(high and breathy)* "Ah'ana, I'm so sleepy."
"Ah'ana, I'm so sleepy."

"Well, let's go to bed now.

It must be the end of the day now, he's become still,"

      they said.

They put their head

which was in a water jar

on the wall, they put it on a shelf.

The mole saw them.

They made their BEDS, the girls made their beds and

      went to SLEEP.

The mole went in, he went in

where their

jar with the head in it was. There were flowers around the

      head

            and the mole pulled the flowers out,

            he pulled all of them out.

He took these outside and gave them to the Payatamu men,

      saying, "You must take all of these, so that his

his flesh will be whole," that's what he said.

                    •

He spoke to the hawk:

      "Now

you must go in," that's what he said. "Very well indeed."

The hawk went in

      lhuuu_uukwa

      he went in.

He took it out, he took the head out quickly.

(high) "Hiyáhha! who has stolen our head?" they said

but he had already taken it out.

The Payatamu men

took their

elder brother's head
wrapped it in a blanket
and went down, they went on down
to the place where he had been killed, with the mole in the lead.

•

He led them on
until they came to the CORNFIELD, came to the cornfield.

•

WHEN THEY GOT THERE
where he had been
killed, lots of flowers were growing.
Lots of flowers were blooming.
"NOW, you must pick all these flowers. When you have
    picked all the flowers, all of them
you will
put them in a bundle."
When they came to where he lay, there were EVEN MORE
    flowers, SO many.
They picked all the flowers until they were all in a bundle,
    in the blanket.
When they had bundled all the flowers
they dug up their elder brother, they dug him up.
They put him on the blanket.

•

They carried their elder brother
going o————n until they got back to their house.
When they got to their house
they laid him on a blanket
a plain one.

They laid their elder brother's body down, laid his head down.

THEY PUT THE FLOWERS ON TOP OF HIM, put the

flowers on top and COVERED HIM WITH

ANOTHER BLANKET.

The PAYATAMU MEN

sat down at their altar.

They sang their string of songs.

They drummed, tesese.

O———n they sang until the first one was finished.

When the second song was finished

he stirred a little.

He stirred

and when the third song was finished he moved a lot.

WHEN THE FOURTH SONG

WAS FINISHED

the Payatamu man ROSE UP.

•

"I'm not even TIRED," that's what he said.

"I'm not even TIRED," he said.

THEIR ELDER BROTHER HAD COME ALIVE, but instead

of a headdress at the back he had a hair knot on his

forehead, he was NEPAYATAMU.

He was saying the opposite of what he MEANT.

•

"I'm not even tired," he said. "Hanaahhhha! our elder

brother, you've come back to life, you are alive

but you are not the same person you were before.

But at least we can SEE YOU."

That's what they said, and

it was now getting LIGHT, it was getting YELLOW, it

was getting to. be MORNING.

Because he had been awakened, the day was COMING.

•

The Nepayatamu man

spoke: "NOW

my younger BROTHERS

•

well

I've come alive, but I'm not the same person.

•

WHAT SHALL WE DO?" THAT'S WHAT he told his

younger brothers.

It was getting light

aaaaaaAAAAAAH THE SUN CAME UP.

When the Sun had come up

Nepayatamu said

"NOW, my younger BROTHERS:

they cannot do WRONG and GET AWAY WITH IT.

We must have REVENGE," that's what Nepayatamu SAID.

When he had spoken, he took out his flute.

Taking his flute

he blew:

such a big swallowtail butterfly

came out.

When it came out it sat down.

So pretty.

•

Then Payatamu
sucked on his flute and the swallowtail went back in.

•

"NOW, we will GO
for they cannot do wrong and GET AWAY WITH IT.
NOW, our GRANDFATHERS

•

RISE UP," he said.
The BEASTS
rose up, the mountain lion

•

the bear
the badger
the mole
the two coyotes lying by the door, all of them came out.

•

Payatamu took them
along with him
he took them o————n until
they arrived at Kyakiima, at the rock
        and when they arrived there he took out his flute
and blew.
The swallowtail came out.
"NOW
this day
you must go where the K'uuchinina People have their home.
When they try to CATCH YOU
you will sprinkle them with your wing powder
and then they can do whatever they wish.

This is what they asked for:
they cannot do wrong and get away with it.
This day we will have revenge," that's what
Nepayatamu told the swallowtail. THE SWALLOWTAIL
    FLEW THERE
going up to where the women had their home, to Kyakiima.
He went there and sat on the ladder. The sunlight
    was coming in
and they saw his shadow: the swallowtail.
Now he came in, came in from perch to perch.
He came down the ladder, so close.
"Wait, don't touch him, we'll look at him
and use his pattern on our basket-plaques," that's
    what they said.

•

The SWALLOWTAIL
flew down to the KILLER HERSELF
and landed on a twig sticking out of the basket-plaque
    she was making.
(high and tight) "Wait, don't touch him, I'll catch him.
When I catch him I'll kill him and we'll use his pattern,
    use his pattern on our basket-plaques," she said.
And the swallowtail landed on a twig that was sticking out.
They were all around him.
He landed on the killer's own stick
    on their elder sister's stick.
She tried to catch him.
He sprinkled them all with his wing powder.

•

THEY WENT CRAZY.

The swallowtail

went up the ladder from perch to perch and they kept
after him until they were all on the roof.

They left their basket-plaques behind.

They kept after him, trying to catch him, hit him, he led them
along toward

Nepayatamu, who was there at their field, up in the
top of a cottonwood tree: Nepayatamu.

He was up there with his flute while they were led along by
the swallowtail, and

they tried to catch him by throwing their capes

and HE LED THEM ALONG UNTIL

they came to the middle of the field
and by now they didn't have any clothes on.

Just NAKED.

They kept after him and he led them ON

to where the cottonwood tree stood
and they all lay down in the shade to rest.

(high and tight) "Ahwa, I'm so tired."

"Me too, so tired."

.

Nepayatamu

spit on them with the owl's root.

The women went to sleep.

.

Now he summoned his grandfathers, "NOW, this day,
grandfathers, enter upon my road," and

they were hiding someplace, the beasts were.

•

They came out
and had pleasure with the flesh of the women, another wrong
    was done, and
this went on

o————n until, when they had all gone, the women awoke.
They were NAKED.
They looked up in the cottonwood tree and saw Nepayatamu

•

sitting there with his legs dangling down.
And when
the swallowtail had come back he had sucked on his flute
and the swallowtail had gone back in.
They found him sitting up there.
"NOW GIVE US SOMETHING IN RETURN," they said.
    "Yes, I'll give you something in return," he said.

•

From the cottonwood
he took leaves.
Wetting these
he threw them down
and they became blankets.
They dressed themselves with these.
He gave each one of them something in return.

•

Nepayatamu came down
    he came down:

    "NOW
this day

I will take you all to my house, to my own house,"
    that's what he said.
"Very well."
Payatamu, Nepayatamu took the lead
while all the beasts dispersed to their shrines.

                        •

He led the women on until they arrived there at
    Shuun Hill, at his house.
His kinswomen
got after the K'uuchinina People:
    "Haa—so these are the
    fools who killed our elder brother.
They're just pitiful things," that's what they told
    them, they got after them.
He brought them in
Nepayatamu
brought the women in.
There were eight of them.

                •

They were led in

                •

and Nepayatamu's kinswomen
Payatamu's kinswomen
were shelling corn.
They were shelling corn, shelling corn
and they put the kernels on the grinding stone

    and made the other women do the grinding.
Those women
stooped over

and they only rubbed the corn, talalala, they couldn't grind
   it, couldn't grind it.
The Payatamu women got angry and said, "You're such big
   women
yet you can't grind it, even though
the kernels aren't hard," but they had done something to the
   kernels so that
they were hard to grind.
They got after them, moved them aside, and did the grinding
   themselves.

                              •

And NEPAYATAMU
got some buckskin and made moccasins for them,
      o———————n until, when four days had PASSED
he had finished eight pairs of moccasins for them.
On the ^{eve} of the ^{FIFTH} day
on the fourth night
porridge was made for them
and meal cakes.

                              •

That night they were all WASHED, their hair was
   washed, their bodies were washed.
They were clothed
the next morning
and had their meal, they were given PLENTY to eat,
   PLENTY to drink.
Nepayatamu said
      "NOW, this day

I will take you to the place where our Sun Father comes out:
because you cannot do wrong and get away with it," that's
what Nepayatamu told the women.

•

To his fathers, his younger brothers, he said, "NOW, my
younger BROTHERS
my KINSWOMEN
you must disappear from this PLACE
and when the time comes at the Middle Place
when it comes at the Middle Place

•

you will be offered prayer-sticks here.
And when the Clown Society becomes known at the
Middle Place
it will be because of me that the Clown Society
comes to be, that's why I
have become the way I am.
THIS DAY I will take these women to the place where
the Sun comes out," that's what he told them.
"VERY WELL." "Yes, that's the way it will be.
And from this place you
must disappear," that's what their elder brother told them.
He took the K'uuchinina women out and led them toward the
place where the Sun comes out
o————n they went

•

and when they had passed Striped Ruin
their
elder sister, the killer, got tired.

She was tired and they tried to help her

but it was no use.

It was no use, she was so tired that she kept falling down,
    falling down, she was thirsty.
"So.

Well, if IT'S NO USE, that's the way it will have to be."
And when he had spoken he sucked on his flute:

the girl went inside.

HE BLEW, and WHITE MOTHS, a whole flock
    of them, came out.

•

"NOW, this is the life you will live, so that when
    spring is near you will be a sign of its coming."
That's what he told the girl.
She became MOTHS.

•

HE TOOK THE OTHERS ALONG AND THEY GOT
    TIRED *(weakly)* and he kept turning them into moths
    and butterflies, on he went
o————n until their youngest sister was the
    only one left.

That one

•

he took along BY FORCE, by force, she was very tired
    but he kept on
and it was no use, she kept falling down and he would
    help her up.
(return to normal voice) "YOU CAN'T MAKE IT?" "No,
    I can't make it, it's no use." "Indeed.

Well, you asked for it
for you were all very foolish."
He sucked on his flute
and the girl went inside the flute.
He blew on it
and out came a whole swarm of moths.
"NOW
this is the life you will live: whenever
winter is near
you will be a sign
that winter is coming."
That's what NEPAYATAMU told her.
THEN HE WAS ALONE
and he went on toward the place where the Sun Father
    comes out.
HE WENT ON THIS WAY until
he came to the ocean
    Nepayatamu came there.

Out in the midst of the waters his father came out, the Sun.
The young man spoke:

        •

"My father, my CHILD, how have you been passing the
    days?" "Happily, my child, so you've come. Now come on
OUT HERE."

        •

That's what he told Nepayatamu, who walked into the water,
    going on to the place where
his father
was coming out.
"NOW, come to my left side and SIT DOWN.

Have you gotten what you WANTED, have you had
    revenge?"
"Yes, I have had my REVENGE.
I wanted to bring them here, but they weren't strong
    enough."
"Indeed, and THAT'S the way it SHOULD HAVE BEEN.
Now, come to me and SIT DOWN.
We shall go and look at the WORLD," and he sat down,
    sat down at his left.
The Sun went on until, around noon
they came here to ZUNI
to the Middle Place.
When they came, there was sprinkling of meal
there was saying of prayers, and some people were doing
    it the right way, while Payatamu
was taken along, at noon.
        When it was noon
his Sun Father said, "NOW
my father, my child
IT IS GOOD that you have come back to life this way.
WHENEVER THE CLOWN SOCIETY BEGINS AT THE
    MIDDLE PLACE, it will be made good because of you.
Now that you have come alive
we will GO
over there to your SHRINE
where I will set you down," that's what he said.
ON THEY WENT UNTIL
they came to ASH WATER
where Nepayatamu was set down.

Nepayatamu was set down there.

That's why, when there is a Clown initiation, they have
the Clown People have
a Milky Way, that's why there's a SOCIETY of
   CLOWN PEOPLE:
when this had happened the CLOWN
   SOCIETY WAS CREATED.
This was lived LONG AGO. Lee————
semkonikya.

NOTES

Narrated by Andrew Peynetsa on the evening of February 23, 1965,
with Walter Sanchez and myself present. The performance took forty-
nine minutes.

K'uuchinina People: eight sisters; according to Andrew, their name is
"an old, old word for women."

Payatamu: Payatamu proper (the protagonist), his four younger broth-
ers, and their kinswomen; together, they form a "medicine society," an
organization with secret methods for performing cures and other won-
ders.

Rock of the Sun: a shrine from which the seasonal movement of the Sun
is observed.

"The society chief sat down facing him": a ceremonial posture, with the
legs of both parties held straight out front and their knees and feet almost
touching.

"Coral's direction": an esoteric term for "south."

Vulture: "shu'tsina," the turkey vulture.

The two coyotes: according to Andrew, the "true" coyote, or coyote proper, eats rabbits, lives in mountains, and has good fur; the "juniper coyote" is smaller and redder, has mangy fur, goes around in flats, is afraid of everything, and eats juniper berries, grasshoppers, and stink-bugs. The mountain lion, bear, and badger are honored by being told to lie near the society's altar, which is on the side of the room farthest from the door; the two coyotes are told to lie near the door because they have little worth.

Tenatsali flowers: these are medicinal and come in various colors, including yellow and blue. Asked to identify tenatsali more precisely, Andrew said, "If you are a medicine man, then you know what kind of medicine that is."

Hawk: "anelhaawa," Cooper's hawk; according to Andrew, "the fastest of all the birds."

Owl: "mewishokkwa," an unidentified species.

"Plain blankets": woven of cotton, white.

The songs: in Andrew's own medicine society (not one of the societies mentioned in this book), this story serves as a prelude and explanation for a song. Andrew refused to record the song.

"Tesese": this is the sound of the pottery drum, a large jar with a skin stretched over its orifice.

Swallowtail butterfly: Andrew used "puulakkya," the generic term for large butterflies, but he meant the Rocky Mountain Swallowtail, with a yellow, blue, and red wing pattern outlined in black. The wing powder of butterflies is an aphrodisiac.

Capes: a pair of scarves, one over the other, tied near the throat and covering the shoulders and back.

"All the beasts dispersed to their shrines": that is, they returned to the places from which they had been summoned.

Corn-grinding: Joseph Peynetsa commented, "A lot of ladies talk about each other. If someone grinds the corn and she can't do a good job, they consider she's not even ready for womanhood. To be efficient, a woman has to be able to do this. If not, she's 'aminne,' good-for-nothing."

Foodstuffs: the porridge is "wolekwiiwe," a paste made from blue corn-meal; the meal-cakes are "he'palokkya," made of whole wheat, something like pancakes but cooked between sheets of cornhusk.

Moths: according to Andrew, the spring and fall moths referred to are both small and white, the only difference between them being that the latter has a larger head. In the story he uses the generic term for moths, "nana pilikkya," literally "grandfather who spills something."

Clown Society: strictly speaking, the Zuni term for this medicine society, "Neweekwe," is an untranslatable proper noun, but Zunis always use "Clown" when talking about this group in English, a reference to the fact that most of its public ceremonies are devoted to satire. The society's members may do or say things which are the opposite of what is logical or proper, just as Nepayatamu did when he said, "I'm not even TIRED." The "Ne-" in "Nepayatamu" is from "Neweekwe."

Milky Way: in Zuni this is "Ash Way"; it is the trail left by Nepayatamu when he travelled across the sky, and the altar of the Clown Society includes a representation of it in the form of a painted board which reaches clear across their room just below the rafters.

THE SUN PRIEST
AND THE WITCH-WOMAN

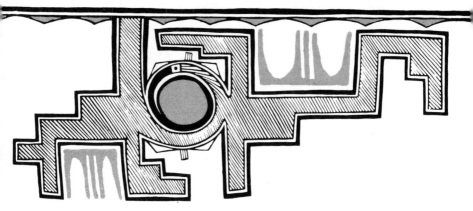

SON'AHCHI.

SONTI ^{LO}————NG A_{GO.}

THERE WERE VILLAGERS AT THE MIDDLE PLACE

•

there were villagers at WIND PLACE
THERE WERE VILLAGERS at Kyakiima
and

•

at Striped Rock
there were two witches:
a witch-girl and her
mother, the two of them, lived alone.
All the VILLAGERS
lived on
and, as usual, there was a PRIEST'S SON

•

whose father knew many prayers.
For this reason
the two witches had bad feelings.
They lived on this way
and whenever a ceremony came up

it was made whole through the thoughts of the Sun Priest.
That girl
SPOKE OUT:
"WHY IS IT
this priest knows so many prayers?
(tight) What should be done
about this? I think
we should shut him off.

 If we shut him off _{we could} do whatever we WAN_{TED}
since we could have a SUN PRIEST of our own.
And perhaps by means of our prayers, well
perhaps by means of our
our PRAYERS, our SUN PRIEST would be the KEEPER
of ALL THIS EARTH, well I
think so anyway: wouldn't it be that way, wouldn't it
 turn out well?" that's what she told her mother.

 •

"Well, it's up to you: if you want this, you must make
 up your mind and set a date.
But
it really wouldn't be the Sun Priest alone
who would think otherwise, for he would surely have allies.
Indeed
there at Hanging Wool
the Ahayuuta
live.
He speaks to them there.
It's up to YOU: if you want this, if this is what you think

if your mind is made up, then
this EVENING
you must make it known to the others. To make it known
we will call a meeting over there
where the White Rocks sit
where some of our houses are.
When we have met
you
will make it known
to your
gathering
what you have in mind, then they will think about it: perhaps

        •

they will be of the SAME MIND with yourself."
That's what
the witch's
mother, the girl's mother
that's what she told her daughter.
And so
they lived on until EVENING.
As SOON as the sun went down
a coyote gave his wets'ots'o cry
he gave his wets'ots'o cry

        •

and the witches among the Zunis HEARD IT.
When they heard it: "Haa——
for what reason are they calling a meeting?"
That's what they said.

Twice there was the wets'ots'o cry.

"It must be urgent."

THAT'S WHAT THE WITCHES SAID
and they went to where the White Rocks sit
the witches.
When they got there
others were going in.
They greeted one another as they went in.
They kept on going in until
everyone was there.
Some time passed
and the Sun Priest

had a witch-friend
who was a young fellow.

He was the one who came in late, he came in late.
Their Bow Priest said, *(tight and closed)* "Why have you come
in so late?"
That's what he asked the boy. "Well
(gently) I didn't hear it right away.
My mother heard it first
and she told me, so that's why I
came in last," that's what
the little boy said. "Indeed.
Did you stop anywhere on the way?" "No, my mother
heard it first, I

didn't hear the meeting called, I didn't hear it

> my mother heard it, that's why I just got here."

The little boy then sat down.

•

Their Bow Priest questioned them: "NOW
for what reason have we been called to a meeting?
Perhaps it is because of a WORD of some importance
that we have been called to a sudden meeting.
WELL NOW, SPEAK UP. WHO IS IT, and what is his

> reason for calling a meeting?" that's what their
> Bow Priest asked them.

•

It was the ones from Striped Rock, the two witches
who lived alone there
who knew about this.
The girl spoke: "IT'S ME, it's because of me
that you have been called to a meeting.
TRULY
we have a SUN PRIEST.
We have our own Sun Priest
and at the Middle Place, they also have their Sun Priest.
At the Middle Place

> it is by the prayers of their Sun Priest, it is by his words

that the villagers live.
But I think that this should not be.
We too have our Sun Priest.
Why isn't our Sun Priest like the one they have at Zuni?
Why isn't he the same kind of person as theirs?

Why is it that theirs is foremost in anything sacred, why is
    he the one who
has the word?'' that's what the girl said.
Their witch, Witch Bow Priest spoke: "YES, in TRUTH
even if THAT'S what you have in MIND
and even if we
did this
together
it wouldn't turn out well for us, because of their Sun Priest:
because of HIS thoughts, the raw people
listen to his words.

                                •

Moreover
whenever the Sun Priest speaks of what must be done
we just follow this, we follow this
in the ceremonies
which include us.
And whenever one of us has meanness in his HEART
that's the time for starting talk
about witching someone:
then we call a meeting, when something WRONG has
    happened.
But what you are talking about now, what you have in mind
    would not turn out well.
What's your reason for thinking
THIS way?
What are we supposed to do?

                                •

If we KILLED THE SUN PRIEST
then this man here would replace him, is that what
    you had in mind, is that why you
called this meeting?"
That's what their Witch Bow Priest said.

•

The little boy sat there with his head down
the little boy thought about their words with his head down.

•

Then it was their
Witch Sun Priest who spoke: "YES, in TRUTH, even if
    that's what you
think about the Sun Priest
I'm NOT WILLING:
I don't know the prayers,

    or how my words could be heard by the raw people.
This wouldn't turn out well for us.
We would be found out quickly.
Certainly
there are the Ahayuuta twins, and
they are wonderful, they are extraordinary persons.
If we made a mist$_a{}_{ke}$
then SURELY
we would be killed.
Then what would happen? After they killed us
could we still carry on?" that's what
their Witch Sun Priest said.

"So I don't agree, but
　　what　　　　thi_n
　　　　　you
　　ₑver　　　　　　k

whatever you think.

WELL NOW, SPEAK, what's this all about?"

　　　　that's what he said.

"Yes, in truth"

the girl said

"I know that

my feelings are not good.

　　　　　　　　　　　•

The way you talked, the way you talked at first

if we killed him

then you would take his place," that's what

the girl said. "Yes, but I'm not willing to do that.

I will not do it.

ALL THE VILLAGERS

are his children.

We are his, even though we are not responsible people.

I do not have all the people as my own.

And if someone makes up his mind, if someone

is sick in his heart

in his heart

(sighing) then that's the time for us to make plans

for whatever we want to do.

But as for you, I won't do it.

However, it's up to YOU

if you are WILLING.

Whatever you have in mind

you will make up your mind to do it.

This night

you must make your plans.

You must SPEAK. If you SPEAK

to the gathering here, then everyone

who is gathered here will think about it," that's what he

said to the witch-girl.

·

"So you AREN'T WILLING.

For THIS I have you as my MENfolk, you here.

If you aren't willing

that's why we two live by ourselves.

That's why

being mere women, we live poorly.

But I will do what I have decided to do.

·

Tomorrow night

·

I will go."

That's what she said, she said. "Indeed.

How will you go?" they said.

·

"I will go as an owl.

When I go as an owl

I will make a trap for the Sun Priest.

Whatever happens then will be up to him," that's what

the girl said. "Indeed.

It's up to YOU, if you want it.

You must do whatever you have DECIDED to do.

You must not waver in your thoughts.

PER^{HAPS, IN SOME} WAY

you will be found out.

If you are KILLED

THAT WILL BE ALL, there is no one among us

who would take pity on you

for that is not our way."

That's what their witch-chief said.

•

"Anyway, THAT'S WHY

I asked you to come. I had REALLY hoped you would all be

willing, but TOMORROW NIGHT I will go by myself,"

that's what she said.

•

"Very well indeed, then let's get some REST.

After a good rest

a person

is better able to kill."

That's what they said. They dispersed.

And the girl

left and went to her home at Striped Rock.

There

she spent the night.

•

The next day

she stayed there all day.

And when they had DISPERSED, the little boy

had left. When he left

•

he went along with the other witches, so he didn't stop
    at his friend's place but went straight home.

•

When he got there
to his house
his mother
was still up.
She was still up when he got there.

(high) "Ahwa, I'm so tired," he said. "Indeed, that was a
    long way.
It wasn't nearby," that's what his mother said.

"For what reason
did they call a meeting?" she said.
"Well
        they're planning to kill the Sun Priest:
the ones
from Striped Rock, those two.
They're the ones: because the Sun Priest
knows so many prayers
their feelings are not good.
It was for this talk of killing him
that we met.
(pained) Because I was late the Bow Priest got after me,
        because I was late."
That's what the little boy said.

    "Yes, just as I THOUGHT:
you stayed too long at your
friend's house.

That's why I told you to hurry, lest

something like this should HAPPEN."
That's what she told him.

"What now:
are you going to tell your friend?" *(high)* "Wait,
I'll go tell him in the morning, for the others
might see me," that's what the little boy said.
"Then you must get up very early," she said. "Yes."

•

They slept through the night, and the NEXT MORNING,
very early, the little boy got up
and went to his friend's, to the Sun Priest's.
He went over to the Sun Priest's house.

"My fathers, my mothers
how did you pass the night?" "Happily, our child, so you've
you've come, sit down," he was told, and he sat down.

•

When he sat down
his
Sun Priest, the one who was to be killed, questioned him:
"NOW
my son, my CHILD
for what reason were you called to a meeting?" he asked him.
(high) "Well
they met to speak of bad things.
They met to speak of bad things:

•

that's why I'm unhappy. I became unhappy
when they spoke out about you:

you who are the Sun Priest
of a———ll the villagers, you who know many prayers.
The raw people listen to your words of prayer.
Moreover, there at Hanging Wool Point
are 'The Two Who Keep The Roof':
that's what they said, whatever they meant,
     'THE TWO WHO KEEP THE ROOF,' " that's what
     the little boy said. "Indeed.
They meant our two fathers: whenever there is the sound
     of an enemy, they're the ones who protect us.
They're very brave"

     that's what
the Sun Priest said.

     "Indeed.
That's the way they talked"
     that's what he said.

     "Indeed.
What are they going to do?
How are they going to kill me, by what means
     are they going to KILL me?"
"With an owl," he said. "Indeed.
Indeed," he said.
"Yes
with an owl.
When night comes
this evening
an owl will come."
That's what the little boy said.

"However

I don't know of any way to help you.
I'm not a knowledgeable person.

        •

It seems I'm not a good person.
It seems I'm a person who doesn't know what's right.
(pained) I didn't know about this
until the wets'ots'o cry was given.
As you know, I was called.
So this is what I am.
I had thought I was the kind of person
who lives the way you do
but I'm

not a good person.

My mother told me to go, and when I got there late *(pained)*
        their Bow Priest got after me because I was late.
'I didn't know about it.
When
your
crier shouted out, I didn't hear it:
my mother told me,' that's what I told him.
        You know I was HERE, don't you,"
        that's what the little boy said. "Yes.
Indeed.

        •

Well, so THAT'S
the bad thing they're thinking.
What have I done, what difficulty have I caused?" that's what
the Sun Priest said.

(pained) "No, nothing, it's because you know
so many prayers
that even the raw people
live by them.
Because you are the one who knows so many prayers
she has bad feelings.
That's why their
Witch Sun Priest
would take your place:
that's what she thinks, but
the one who holds that position doesn't want this, because
he doesn't know all the things you know, that's why he
　　doesn't want this," that's what the boy said. "Indeed.
Let them do whatever they want with ME.
If they would KILL me, let one of them take my place.
But there is CLANSHIP:

　　　　　　　　　•

THIS is the institution by which I live.
Clanship does not exist for no REASON, clanship
is not an unimportant institution.
Only a member of the DOGWOOD Clan should be the Sun
　　Priest."
That's what
the Sun Priest said
　　that's what he said.
(high) "Anyway, that's what they talked about," he said.
　　"Indeed.
Very well indeed. WHEN

WILL IT COME?" "When the sun goes down"
that's what he said.

"Indeed.
Then are you
going to STAY HERE?" that's what he asked him.
"No, I'll
go, if I stayed
they might find out somehow, and if something happened
if you killed her and I stayed here and they saw me
then, if they had another meeting and I went there,
   they would hold it against me. I'm going
I'm leaving," that's what the little boy said.
"Very well indeed. Those Two you talked about:
I'm going to their house at Hanging Wool.

•

THAT'S WHERE I'M GOING TO SPEND THE NIGHT,
   LET THE OWL COME HERE,"
   that's what the Sun Priest said.
That's what the Sun Priest said.
The little boy

•

left, and because he didn't want to be found out he went
   around, went all around before he went to his house.
The Sun Priest left.
   When the Sun Priest left

•

he went to Hanging Wool.
When he came to Hanging Wool
where the Ahayuuta lived
the Ahayuuta twins were sitting up on their roof.

·

"My two fathers, my two children, how have you been

   passing the days?" "Happily, our father,

   so you've come."
That's what they said.

   "Yes, I've come to talk with you."

   "Indeed. Then let's go inside," they said.
They took him inside, the Sun Priest.
When they took him inside

their grandmother was MAKING PORRIDGE.
Their grandmother was making porridge.

·

"My mother, my child, how have you been passing the days?"

   "Happily, our father, so you've come, be seated,"

   he was told.
They put out a seat for him and he sat down.

·

"SON," that's what
she said
to the elder
of the Ahayuuta brothers. "What is it?"
"Make a cigarette," that's what
she said
to the boy.
Her grandson made a cigarette.
He made a cigarette
and when he had finished

·

he sat down facing the Sun Priest. When he sat down facing him

·

he took Grandmother Fire by the arm

drew her forward

and lit the cigarette, lit it.

He sent mist in all directions, strengthening hearts, and blew
smoke on himself.

He gave it to the Sun Priest.

The Sun Priest also sent mist in all directions, strengthening
hearts, and blew smoke on himself.

He questioned him then

•

the Ahayuuta did:

"NOW

our FATHER

for what reason

have you entered upon our roads? Perhaps it is because
of a WORD of some importance

that you have entered upon our ROADS. You would not
do this for no REASON.

You would not come to talk with us for no reason,
that's not your way

for it is through your words of prayer that we listen to YOU.

It is CERTAIN

that every DAY

you give us PRAYER-MEAL

you make OFFERINGS.

The Uwanammi WATER-PRIESTS

a————ll over the wide EARTH

the RAW PEOPLE

wherever they stay, they listen to your words of prayer.

So it must be for a WORD of some importance that you
enter upon our roads.

YOU MUST MAKE THIS KNOWN TO US
so that we may think about it
as we pass the days, IS IT NOT SO?" he said to his
    younger brother. "IT IS SO," he said.
Their grandmother also said, "It is so."

      •

"YES, in TRUTH, my fathers, my CHILDREN:
there at the MIDDLE PLACE
the ones who do not know what is right

      •

had a meeting last night.
When they met last night

for some reason
they talked about killing me.
They thought of killing me, and TONIGHT
an owl will come, perhaps it will kill me.
That's what my friend
told me this morning.
That's why
I came out this way, to ask you
whether there is some way to make this turn out well,"
    that's what
the Sun Priest said.
"Indeed.
It will turn out WELL, our FATHER
you must not WORRY.
You must not waver in your THOUGHTS.
They have ASKED FOR IT.

It is CERTAIN
that many of your LIFE-seeds
have been DESTROYED by them.
They do not follow the RIGHT WAY."
That's what
the Ahayuuta
said to the Sun Priest.
"That's why
I have COME.
Perhaps you might tell me something to make it turn out well.
Perhaps
they will not kill me.
       IF THEY KILL ME,   someone
And   perhaps there is
who would take my place. This clanship I live by:
even those who don't know what is right
have their clanship. If someone were willing
he could take my place.
A————ll
our children, where the ladders descend:
like them
you who are our fathers
you have
brave hearts, all of us have brave hearts"
          that's what the Sun Priest said.

       "Yes.
This is the way you live," the Ahayuuta twins said.
                              •

"But WAIT," that's what their grandmother said
          the twins' grandmother.

"Father-child, you must wait"
 she said.

　　　　　　　　•

"Let me prepare you," that's what she said, and she went into
　　the next room. She went in

　　　　　　　　•

and brought out a bow.
　　She brought out a bow and laid it down, then got a quiver.

"Prepare THIS for him"
she told them, and gave
an arrow to them
to the twins.
She gave it to her grandsons and they prepared it.
They
prepared it with honey.

　　　　　　　　•

"NOW, you must take this along.
You must take this along
and
you mustn't get sleepy before the OWL COMES. The owl will
　　surely land
at the top of the LADDER.

　　　　　　　　•

Then it will make itself known to the others
with a huhhu.
When it ^makes itself ^known with a ^huhhu
the others will start coming down.
They will come ^down there around your ^house

while it sounds FOUR TIMES.

It will sound the first time, the second time

and when it sounds the third time

you must put this arrow

on your bow.

THE ^{FOURTH} TIME IT SPEAKS

you will shoot it for them.

When you have shot THEIRS

LEAVE THE ARROW IN IT

and throw it down to them.

'NOW, here is your life-seed, PICK IT UP.

You asked for THIS.

You may take it away,' that's what you will tell them.

Then they can do whatever they wish.

•

TOMORROW

as soon as the sun comes up

when you have brought your Sun Father out

you must not go back

to your house

but must come here.

Then we will tell you

what to do next," that's what

the Sun Priest

was told

that's what they told him. "Indeed.

Very well." "Yes, that's the way it will be.

(kindly) You must not WORRY.

You must not waver in your thoughts.

There may be people who do wrong

but

you ask for daylight for everyone.

You say prayers even for the one who is not upright.

You pray for everyone.

If someone

•

is not a good person, that is unfortunate.

But IT WILL TURN OUT WELL if they want it that way.

TOMORROW, when you come back, we will know what

to do, *(pained)* but don't make a MISTAKE.

You must not WORRY.

If you WOR_{RY}

this thing we've prepared for you won't work," that's what

the Ahayuuta grandmother said.

"If you WORRY, you won't do it right. Don't waver

in your thoughts.

Be just the way you are right now:

if you feel this way

then you will do it right

then it will turn out well"

that's what she said.

"There is your

friend:

certainly

•

he'll be in this, for his mother has spoken to him,
  and certainly he'll be in this with you,"
  that's what she said.

                    •

"Are you
(serious) on good speaking terms with him?" "Yes. Well
yes I am, and I'm
always kind to him, as if he were my own child.
I'm always kind to him. When he was a small boy
his elders
spoke to me
about us:
they spoke to me about it, that's why we pledged our
  friendship.
We didn't just WASH each other to pledge friendship,
  it wasn't
like that.

                    •

I gave him a beaded necklace. When I gave him
  a beaded necklace
his elders
gave me a blanket:
THAT'S the way I pledged friendship with him, with my
my child.
I value him," that's what he said. "Certainly
that's the way it should be," that's what the Ahayuuta
  grandmother said.
(kindly) "WELL THEN, our father, have good thoughts, don't
think about this bad talk you've heard, leave it behind you.

•

YOU MUST GO HAPPILY upon the pollenway, you must
    think well of what you are going to do.
That way
you can do it right.
WE WILL KNOW ABOUT IT, for we will go there also.
You will not be alone"
      that's what they said, the Ahayuuta twins.
"We will watch over you:
you won't be alone," they said.

•

The man
the Sun Priest was leaving. "Very well, I'm going."
"You must put this in your
quiver:
you must take along what we have prepared for you
and when
you kill the owl with it, you must leave it in when you
    throw the body down to them, and when they take it out
we'll get it back," that's what they said. "Very well."
"Yes, that's the way it will be."
"Very well indeed, I'm going
my children
may you have a good day and evening." "Indeed, may
    it be the same with you, our father"
      they said.

•

The Sun Priest took his arrow
and went back to Zuni, to the Middle Place.

It was almost sunset
when he got there.
When he got there

           •

he was fed. When he was fed
his wife

and his children ate with him.

His wife questioned him

    and he told them
what he had been told by the Ahayuuta.

           •

"We'll see what happens. If I
know how, I will kill theirs.
Tomorrow
I have to go back
     that's what they told me

and tonight
the Ahayuuta will come here.
From somewhere they will watch over me.
I won't be alone, that's what they told me."

"Very well indeed."
They ate
their evening meal a little early. They waited and
    the sun went down.

           •

Time went o————n until it was late

           •

then

sure enough, by the ladder

they heard it plainly,

kolo

as the owl alighted.

"So, it must've come."

•

Some time passed

then the owl gave its huhhu:

"Hu

huHU

hu"

it said.

"Haa——, sure enough, it's come."

And a second time

it spoke:

again, again it gave the huhhu.

It was not to finish speaking.

"Hu hu."

•

When it had spoken a third time

just as he had been told, he stood by the ladder.

Sitting up there was the owl.

He put the arrow on his bow

and when it was about to give another huhhu

po$_o$$_o$$_o$
$_{ok'o}$

he shot it.

The owl fell.

•

The Sun Priest hurried out

and picked it up.

It was dead.

The arrow was sticking in the owl but he didn't take it out,

just as he had been told.

He threw it down to them:

there were a lot of people below, sure enough:

the witches.

•

"Here, take your

child"

that's what he told them.

•

They dispersed.

They passed the night

and the next day, before the sun came up

he started back.

He brought out his Sun Father, then went back to the Ahayuuta.

The Ahayuuta twins

were sitting up on top when he got there.

"My two children, how did you pass the night?" "Happily,

our father, so you've come back." "Yes, I've come

back." *(high and hoarse)* "Then let's go inside," they said.

They went inside, and their

grandmother was MAKING PORRIDGE AGAIN.

She was making porridge

when they came in.

"My mother, how did you

pass the night?" "Happily, our father

so you've come back." "Yes, I've come."

"It's good that you've come.
It will turn out well for you"
        that's what she said.

        •

"NOW
our father, our child

        •

(serious) be seated

        •

for tonight
they will surely have another meeting.
The ones who started this talk:
THIS VERY DAY
we will have a contest with them.
Perhaps they are surpassing people," that's what the
        Ahayuuta grandmother said
that's what she told him. "Indeed.
Indeed," the Sun Priest said. "Yes.
Now, my two GRANDSONS
make preparations for our father," that's what
the Ahayuuta grandmother
said to her two grandsons.

        •

The twins took out their quiver, took out their quiver
        and prepared four arrows, prepared them with honey.
There was a very BROAD spearhead.
They put that
in their quiver.

        •

"And what about this:

·

the one that
our Sun Father
gave us, should we take it along?" they asked their
    grandmother.
"Yes, you must take that along.
Perhaps it will make things easier," she said.
It was a TURQUOISE CLUB.
This is what the Sun, their Sun Father, had given them, and
    they had been keeping it.
THEY PUT THIS IN THEIR QUIVER ALSO. "Now let's
    go," they said.

·

They went out.
"NOW
this day, our father, our mother

we'll GO ON THE ROAD NOW.
We'll see how this day turns out," they said.
    "Very well, you may go, we'll see how this day turns out.

DON'T you make any MISTAKES," they were told.
They went across toward Striped Rock.
They went across

going on until they came to
a point, a rocky point overlooking Striped Rock
and sat down on top of it.
There, down below, smoke was coming out of their house.
Smoke was coming out.

·

"Is that their house?"

"Yes, that's the house where they live.

Wa————y over there is their cornfield," that's what he said. "Indeed."

(aside) It was where a small arroyo came out, that's where

they had their field.

•

Soon, the woman came out and went to her cornfield. After

a while, her mother came out and went there also.

"Now let's go," they said.

They went down

went on down

until they were close

to their house. Meanwhile the women were going about in their

cornfield, they were hoeing.

•

It was the elder of the Ahayuuta brothers who said, "Wait now.

How should we do this? Should we

destroy their house first?" he said.

His younger brother said

"Don't.

Let's alarm them, so that

they'll go inside.

As soon as they go inside

then we'll kill them," that's what he said.

"All right," he said.

His younger brother

sat down

(aside) beneath a tree.

When he sat down: "NOW, this day

our father, who lives with us

the mountain lion:

now enter upon my road," that's what the Ahayuuta said
    that's what the Ahayuuta said.

                    •

After a while

the mountain lion

    came.

He came to where they were waiting.

    The women were still at their cornfield

going about hoeing.

The mountain lion came up and said, "My fathers, my children,
    how

have you been?" "Happy, our

father-child, so you've come now."

"Yes."

"NOW, for what reason have you summoned ME?

Perhaps it is because of a WORD of some importance that

    you have summoned me," that's what he told them.

"YES, in TRUTH

                    •

our GRANDFATHER, our FATHER, our CHILD

it concerns our father here, the Sun Priest: a————ll

    you raw people

listen to his words of prayer and live by them.

He offers you hard things

he offers you prayer-meal.

Because of this, there was talk of KILLING him.

Last night

                    •

he was supposed to have been killed by an owl
and so
he came to our house
to ask what he should do.
This day
we will KILL the women who live here, this is the house
    of the ones who started the talk of killing him.
Over there they are going about in their field.
I was going to call out in imitation of you
(low and gravelly) but perhaps I wouldn't have done it well:
that's why I summoned you.
When you make your sound
and they hear you
THEY'LL RUN
THEY'LL GO INSIDE
then we'll kill them, THAT'S WHAT
we have in mind, that's why we've come here," that's
    what he said. "Indeed.
It should turn out well, certainly.
We listen to the prayers of our father here, and live by
    them."
"Indeed. So this is what has happened.
Because of the thoughts of these two
this has happened.
THAT'S why we'll kill them.
This NIGHT
we'll go to White Rocks, for the others will certainly
    have a meeting," that's what

·

the Ahayuuta said. *(low)* "Indeed. Very well indeed,
then I'll alarm them." *(high)* "Go ahead and alarm
them, and we'll see what they do.

Now, our father, we'll
set you up here," they said, and they took their
turquoise club and SET IT UP.

When they set it up
they looked at it.

(tight) "This won't do for me.

It's too close
too close for me. Why don't you set it up a little
further back?

That'll be better for me.

I'll be last in line, I won't step beyond the club,"
that's what
the mountain lion said.

(high and hoarse) "Yes, yes, WAIT, LET'S
set it up there"

(aside) and they moved further back and set up their
turquoise club.

Some distance behind them the mountain lion got down
on all fours.

(low and gravelly) He gave his tuwoo, tuwoo.

they heard it

THEY CAME RUNNING!!
they CAME RUNNING and went inside their house.

•

The Ahayuuta twins went and stood there
beside their door.

The Sun Priest

the one who was to have been killed stood in their

    doorway *(aside)* and the two Ahayuuta got behind him.

The mountain lion

got behind them.

They stood there before the house.

•

"So you've COME now, so you've COME now"

    that's what she said. "Yes."

"Indeed.

so you've come.

For what reason have you COME?

What do you mean by COMING HERE?" THAT'S WHAT

    THE WITCH-GIRL'S

mother said. "Indeed.

Well, ON THE NIGHT you called a meeting

you wanted to kill me, that's why

THIS DAY

•

it will be our turn to kill YOU.

Because

I stand first among you, you wanted to have your

Witch Sun Priest

take my place, you thought of doing wrong.

You made up your mind.

I asked help

from my two fathers here.

THIS DAY

since you asked for it
we will end your daylight.
TO^{NIGHT THE O}THERS WILL MEET
AND we will kill all of them there.
WHEN ALL OF YOU ARE FINISHED
THEN we will have ONE WAY of thinking as we live.
We will not have bad feelings toward one another.
IT'S TRUE that you have your GARDEN SEEDS
and where all the ladders descend there is good flesh
BUT you have been very foolish.
SO I have made up my MIND.
Even though you are not good
I HAVE ASKED DAYLIGHT FOR YOU *(tight)* but it seems
    you want SOMETHING MORE.
THAT'S WHY, on this day
you will pass away.
Over there
when the others meet, we will kill them ALL," that's
    what the Sun Priest said
to the witches.
They didn't want it.
"YES, we will kill you.

                            •

LOOK AT YOUR SUN FATHER FOR THE LAST TIME,"
    that's what the Sun Priest said.

                            •

They put their
arrows

the ones that had been prepared, on their bows

> and the twins shot them

they shot them.

WHEN THEY SHOT THEM they both died.

The twins spoke to their turquoise club:

"NOW

our father-child

you will strike them a second time, for they aren't really dead
> yet"

> that's what they said.

They released their turquoise club, so

and this time

he struck their hearts.

Then they were dead.

"So, we've DONE IT. NOW, our GRANDFATHER, our
> father-CHILD

you must destroy their house," that's what they told the
> mountain lion.

The mountain lion went up, went up on the roof

and started digging.

> As he dug

he threw down the rafters and completely ruined their house.

When ALL THE RAFTERS had fallen in:

"Let's go now."

But first, the Ahayuuta said

to the mountain lion: "NOW, our grandfather, our child

well

that's why we needed you, now you may go back to your
> SHRINE.

When NIGHT comes
we will be without you:
we
will KILL THEM."
That's what
they told the mountain lion. "Very well indeed.
GO RIGHT AHEAD and do it, but I will say THIS to YOU:

•

you
have done wrong.
You must make prayer-sticks.
All your children, where the ladders descend:
if they are to be valued
you must make these prayer-sticks.

•

There
at Corn Mountain
at the SPRING there
you must plant these prayer-sticks
so that
where all the ladders descend, your children
our fathers
will be safe.
For you will have destroyed many lives.

•

That's why you must make prayer-sticks.
You must SET A DATE.
At NIGHT
and in the DAY
you must think of this.

On the FOURTH night

in one house

in your house

you must make preparations.

When you have made prepara~tions~

THEN

we will

make it known

to your daylight children.

Of A————LL your village children, the POOR PEOPLE
    will be the only ones left.

                            •

By means of OUR thoughts

A————LL of us will watch over you from the shrines
    where we live, all around.

ALL OF US   will go   down there

to your house.

When this 'GOOD NIGHT' comes

then we will make

a medicine society for you.

YOUR THOUGHTS WILL BE ROOTED IN THIS as you
    live.

Wherever there is someone who DOESN'T KNOW WHAT
    IS RIGHT

someone who thinks in another way

then by means of OUR medicine, by means of OUR thoughts

you will see

that wrongdoer.

THAT'S

what the GAME will be."

THAT'S WHAT

the mountain lion told the Sun Priest.

"Very well." "Yes, that's the way it will be.

YOU MUST MAKE PREPARATIONS and wait.

WHEN THE TIME COMES

we will go there," that's what

the mountain lion said. "Very well." "Yes, that's the
    way it will be."

"Very well, then you must go."

"Well, I'll be GOING, my fathers, my children, may you
    have a good day and evening."

"May you also have a good day."

Then the Ahayuuta twins

took the Sun Priest to their house.

When they got to Hanging Wool

when they got to Hanging Wool

their grandmother

was waiting when they got there.

When they entered:

"My grandmother, how have you been?"

    "Happy, so you've come back."

"Our mother, our child, how have you been?" "Happy,
    so you've come, be seated," she said.

When they sat down

(with pleasure) THEIR GRANDMOTHER SET OUT A
    MEAL.

She fed them
> their grandmother fed them. They ate

and ate

and when they were full:

"Thanks." "Eat plenty"
> that's what she said.

•

When the meal had been cleared away
she sat down facing him, the Ahayuuta grandmother did.
She sat down facing the Sun Priest. "NOW, this day

•

you have set forth
on your pollenway.
Did you do what you INTENDED to do?" "Yes, we've
> killed both of them. Our
grandfather, the mountain lion, destroyed their house.
THIS NIGHT
we will go
to the others
and KILL THEM too.
After we have killed them
TOMORROW I will work on the prayer-sticks:
that's what our grandfather
the mountain lion
told us, is it not so?" "It is so, that's what he said"
> that's what the Ahayuuta twins said.

•

"SO THEN
you will do this, and it will turn out well.

OTHERWISE it would NOT turn out WELL.

That's what we told you at the START.

                        •

You

                        •

must get the WORD around

to ALL the raw people.

WHEN YOU HAVE GOTTEN THE WORD _{TO THEM}

you will offer them prayer-meal

offer them hard things.

When they come to your house

this will be the 'GOOD NIGHT.'

EVERYONE IN THE VIL_{LAGE MUST BATHE,}

    you must tell them that.

EVEN _{IF THEY} ^{DON'T} WANT TO ^{GO} TO

    YOUR _{HOUSE}

they must bathe.

THEN THE ^{RAW} PEOPLE, WITH THEIR

    UN^{KNOWABLE PO}_{WERS}

    will pluck out whatever is inside them.

That's the way it will be.

HERE^{AFTER}

this is the way our daylight children will live.

And these Ahayuuta twins, who live as Bow Priests:

they will DEPART from here.

These Bow Priest twins will bring the Saniyakya

    Society to light.

Also the Society of Bow Priests will become known.
BECAUSE OF THEIR THOUGHTS
you will live with brave hearts."
That's what the Ahayuuta grandmother
told the Sun Priest
that's what she told him.
"Very well." "Yes, that's the way it will be.
You must have good thoughts."
"VERY WELL INDEED, now I must GO, my FATHERS,
     my MOTHER, my CHILDREN
may you have a good day and evening." "By all means may
     it be the same with you."

                    •

He left, and when he left the little Ahayuuta
followed him: "WAIT, father," he said.
"What is it?" he said.
(high) "When
the SUN GOES DOWN, you will leave your HOUSE

                    •

and we will START OUT
and get there first
and I will give the *(gravelly)* WETS'OTS'O CALL,"
     THAT'S WHAT THE LITTLE AHAYUUTA SAID.
(high and hoarse) "Because the one who had been
     calling them together is already dead
I will be the one to give the wets'ots'o
          haps   h
     per   I'll know ᴼw."
     that's what the younger brother Ahayuuta said.

(smiling) "VERY WELL." "Yes, that's the way it will be.
Now you may go," he said.
The Sun Priest returned to his home.

He stayed there until the sun went down.
After they had eaten
the Sun Priest went out, he went out and went on his way.

THERE was the WETS'OTS'O, the COYOTE.
It was the little Ahayuuta
giving the wets'ots'o.

•

The Sun Priest went on
    went on until
he had passed the witches' houses.
On a small hill
the Ahayuuta
were waiting.

    "Come on over, here we are"
        that's what they said.
They waited there

• and the witches began ARRIVING, SURE ENOUGH.
They were arriving
and entering.
They waited outside for some time
until there was no one else.
But his friend DIDN'T COME
his friend didn't come.

•

IT GREW VERY LATE, but his friend didn't come.
"Your friend hasn't come," that's what the Ahayuuta said.

"No, he hasn't come yet."

"I wonder why he hasn't come, or maybe he's on his way."

"Well no, his mother must've told him not to come," that's
what the elder brother Ahayuuta said.

"He must've been told not to come."

(high and hoarse) "Perhaps he'll be the only one
left, and maybe

he'll go the right way.

With his garden seeds, perhaps all our children,
where the ladders descend

will go the right way.

Let him be spared," that's what the Ahayuuta said.

"NOW LET'S GO," they said.

•

"You must enter first, and when you enter
we will stand behind you. Here is our
turquoise club:
you must set it up in front of you.
And this spearhead:
you will set it up also.

•

You will speak to them
about the contest.
When you have spoken
and they have answered you: 'You should be first,
because you wanted to kill me.
You should be first.

•

You must try to kill me first. Then, if you don't
kill me, perhaps I'll kill you,' " that's what

the Sun Priest

was to say:

that's what they told him to do.

THEY ENTERED.

       When they entered

             •

the Sun Priest

came down

to the foot of the ladder:

"My fathers, my CHILDREN

how are you this evening?" he said.

"Happy, our father, so you've come

SIT DOWN.

We had just gathered when you came in," THAT'S

       WHAT THEY TOLD HIM.

             •

The Ahayuuta twins stood behind him and nobody saw them.

They stood behind his back.

The Sun Priest spoke: "NOW

my children

FOR WHAT REASON

did you want to KILL me?

THIS NIGHT we will have a CONTEST.

YOUR medicine is strong

but even though I am just a POOR person

I am WILLING."

That's what he told them.

"Indeed. Well then

you should be FIRST"

that's what their

Witch Bow Priest said. "Oh no

I will not be first.

.

YOU WILL BE FIRST BECAUSE YOU ARE
        THE WONDER-WORKERS.

.

IF I DON'T DIE

then I might

do something to you, even though I am a POOR person.

Do whatever you wish to ME.

THEN you will be HAPPY," that's what the Sun Priest told
        them.

.

Their witch-chief said, "VERY WELL INDEED, we will
        go FIRST if you are WILLING."

The Ahayuuta said, *(whisper)* "Now hurry:

set up your turquoise club

set up your spearhead," that's what

the Ahayuuta twins told him, from behind his back.

Now he set them up, set up the turquoise club

.

set up the spearhead.

"Ready?" he asked them.

"Now," they said.

The ones in the first row released their

weapons, k'u-cha-cha-cha-cha-cha————

and where he stood

cactus needles and other things fell down.

The SECOND row, the THIRD, the FOURTH row then
released theirs.

•

•

•

"IS THAT ALL?" he said. "OUR WEAPONS are all
gone," they said. "Indeed.
Very well."

"Now it's your turn."

•

He picked up his turquoise club:

"NOW, this night, my father, my child
you must kill all of them

you must not spare anyone.
Let all of them be killed," that's what he told it.

•

The Ahayuuta told it, *(high)* "If anyone is left, well, make
sure no one is left," that's what he said.

The Sun Priest spoke to them again.

•

HE RELEASED HIS TURQUOISE CLUB, and it went
around the first time
the second, the third, IT WENT AROUND THE FOURTH
TIME
and the turquoise club was then taken
by the Ahayuuta.

•

"You must pick up the spearhead and go around
	carefully. You must circle all around until you have
	come back to your starting point."

			•

That's what the Ahayuuta said.

	There was blood

			•

there was blood all around NOW, blood.
"You must be wary as you go around," that's what
	they told him
		that's what the twins told him.
He went on and on and on among the corpses
		but he didn't see anyone left.
"They're all gone now."
"Well, now our worries are ended.
That's all there is to the contest, our FATHER.
You must go happily on the pollenway, and just as
our grandfather said
you must make prayer-sticks tomorrow"
		that's what they said.
	"Very well."
The Ahayuuta twins said, "We're GOING, may you have a
	good night." "Very well
	may it be the same
with you, may you have a good night," that's what he told the
	twins.
They LEFT, then he went to his house.
THE NEXT DAY he cut PRAYER-STICKS, the PRIEST.
The Sun Priest cut sticks.

·

When they were finished

·

he planted the sticks
at Circling Water
at the spring.
HE SET A DATE.
Each night, then
he said prayers
alone.
When the eve of the ceremony came
the Sun Priest summoned his Bow Priest
     he summoned his Bow Priest.
The Bow Priest came to his house.

·

"NOW, for what reason have you summoned me? Perhaps it
    is because of a WORD of some importance"
    that's what he said.

    "YES, in TRUTH
my father, my CHILD
you are our village CHIEF.
You live by the dry bow," that's what he said. "YES,
    in truth, that's the way I LIVE."
That's what he said.

"THIS NIGHT
you will make it known to your children that
    without exception
they will bathe tomorrow, without exception
    they must bathe their bodies

EVEN if they don't come to my house, 'e ven if they stay in
their own houses.

Our fathers

the BEAST PRIESTS

will come.

They will look ALL AROUND AMONG US.

BECAUSE OF THOSE WHO DON'T KNOW WHAT'S
RIGHT, WE MAY BE SICK

and they will remove this from us. BECAUSE OF THIS

because the medicine societies will become known

you will tell your children

that I have set a DATE.

This is the THIRD day. TOMORROW NIGHT

they will come."

That's what he said. "You will speak of this

when you make the announcement to your children"

he said.

"Very well."

"Yes, that's the way it will be."

•

HE LEFT and

shouted it out

telling them to bathe.

The next night

the beasts would come, that's what he said as he announced it.

He shouted it out.

IN KEEPING WITH THE WORDS OF THE
ANNOUNCEMENT, EVERYONE IN THE

VIL LAGE BATHED, EVEN THOSE WHO DIDN'T

GO TO HIS HOUSE

but stayed home.

They lived on, and WHEN THE SUN WENT DOWN

•

the beasts CAME.

They had their medicine water.

They came

and entered the Sun Priest's house.

The mountain lion was first, then the bear

badger

wolf

eagle

mole:

they came in single-file.

•

After a time

their Bow Priest came in:

the white bear.

•

"My fathers, my children, how are you this evening?"

"Happy, our fathers, so you've come now, BE SEATED,"

they said, and their

•

ROOM was BARE.

They sat down.

When they sat down, they set up their

altar, and

a meal painting

•

•

they made a meal painting

they set up their corn ears, set out their medicine water

when they sat down.

•

They sang their string of songs.

They sang their string of songs o————————n

and when their songs were almost finished

•

their

chief got up

    got up while they were still singing and went

    around, went around

  and when he had gone around the fourth time

•

then his younger brothers got up and walked around,

    walked around, laying bare what was inside the

    villagers. And they

asked for a bowl, they were given a bowl, and that's

    where they PUT THINGS.

A lot of

sickness was put in there.

When it was getting light, when day was coming:

    "Perhaps this will DO.

This is about all we can do, for we must not stay

    until the sun comes up:

that wouldn't be good"

    they said.

THOSE people were the REAL raw people.

This is the way the medicine societies were to be:
THAT'S WHAT HAD HAPPENED.
And HIS FRIEND was spared: just as
the Ahayuuta twins had said, his mother had TOLD HIM
    not to go:
that's why his friend was left out.
IT IS BY HIS GARDEN SEEDS, today it is by these
    garden seeds
that we LIVE.
THIS WAS LIVED LONG AGO. *(aside)* Lee————
semkonikya.

NOTES

Narrated by Andrew Peynetsa on the evening of March 10, 1965, with his wife, several other members of his family, Walter Sanchez, and myself present. The performance took fifty-seven minutes.

"As usual, there was a PRIEST'S SON": two nights before this, Andrew had told two stories (not published here) in which the protagonist was a priest's son.

Sun Priest: the highest-ranking of all Zuni priests, keeper of the calendar; he greeted the Sun Father every morning with offerings and prayers. According to Andrew, "He was supposed to keep out of arguments. He wasn't supposed to kill anything, or even step on an ant." The office is now vacant; its duties have been assumed by the second-ranking priest.

Ahayuuta: twin boys, sons of the Sun, protectors of the Zuni people; "The Two Who Keep The Roof," an esoteric name for them, refers to the fact that the surface of the earth forms the roof of four lower worlds. According to Joseph Peynetsa, "The Ahayuuta have long hair and they're dirty; they sort of look like sheepherders." In the "long ago" they lived with their maternal grandmother.

Witches: motivated by jealousy or grudges, they cause illness and death, principally by magically shooting foreign objects into the bodies of their victims. In former times, at least, they were organized into a clandestine medicine society and had a Bow Priest and Sun Priest of their own; any member could call a meeting by giving the coyote call.

Clanship: the Zunis are divided into a dozen clans; membership is inherited through the mother.

The cigarette: wild tobacco, rolled in a cornhusk. The full ritual phrase for lighting a cigarette is, "He took his grandmother by the arm and made her sit down in the doorway," but in the present instance Andrew switches to ordinary language after "by the arm." I supplied "Fire" in making the translation so that Grandmother Fire would not be confused with the Ahayuuta grandmother. The "mist" sent in all directions "strengthens the hearts" of the raw people.

"All our children, where the ladders descend": this refers to the villagers (daylight people), as does "life-seeds."

Honeyed arrows: these are effective against witches; ordinary arrows are not.

"Pollenway": life.

Offerings: "hard things" and "prayer-meal" both refer primarily to a mixture of corn-meal with crushed turquoise, shell, and coral.

The killing of the witches: witches are difficult to kill, and that is why the girl and her mother were struck twice; the girl, in fact, had already been "killed" once before, when she came as an owl.

"You have done wrong": the mountain lion tells the Sun Priest this because it is wrong to take human life, even a witch's life; Joseph explained, "To save himself and his village children, the Sun Priest had to plant feathers, so that perhaps their lives would be spared. It doesn't mean forgiveness—in the white man's way it would say he prays for forgiveness—he did it so that his children would be 'aatehya' [valued], free from evil thoughts, the evil."

"The POOR PEOPLE will be the only ones left": that is, people who lack the powers of witches.

Saniyakya Society: also called the Coyote Society; a medicine society for hunters.

Society of Bow Priests: this formerly consisted of all Zunis who had killed an enemy; the Bow Priest proper, mentioned in this and other stories, was a member.

Beast Priests: the first six come from the six directions (in the story their sequence is north, west, south, east, zenith, nadir); the seventh (the white bear) represents the middle. They are the chief patrons of several medicine societies, and in the story they themselves form a society, with an altar (an enclosure of painted slats with a wooden mobile suspended above it), a meal painting (made on the floor, with corn-meal), etc.

"Good Night": an annual ceremony, at the winter solstice, in which the medicine societies cure, without charge, any villagers who come to the society houses; the medicine men are even able to see and remove the sickness in people who do not present themselves in person. On the first Good Night, in the story, "the REAL raw people" came to do the curing; today their human representatives do it.

"It is by these garden seeds that we LIVE": this refers to yellow corn, which was brought from the underworld at The Beginning by the first witch; if all the witches had been killed, including the Sun Priest's friend, it would have meant the death of yellow corn.

PELT KID AND HIS GRANDMOTHER

SON'AHCHI. THERE WERE VILLAGERS AT THE
    MIDDLE PLACE
and
PELT KID LIVED WITH HIS GRANDMOTHER.
    (tries to suppress laughter)

                        •

They were living together this way, and at the Middle Place
the villagers
came down to get water
at their
well
and that Pelt Kid was very stupid, he just didn't know
    anything.
One night when they were still up
he told his grandmother

    "Tomorrow, I
would like to gather wood."
That's what he told his grandmother. "Well, you may go
for we're almost out of wood," she said.
"Then we should
get some rest," that's what he said, and

they slept through the night, and the next day his
   grandmother
got up, then
she made some corn-cakes and they ate. When they had eaten
   he
put his rolled-up thongs on his back and
went down
      went on down toward the south.
Before he left, his grandmother
had told him:
"Grandson, when you
gather wood, when the tree
falls
you must run away from it," that's what his
   grandmother had told him.
"Well then
I'll try to do that," he had said.
He went on until
he came to where a dried-up tree stood, and he started
      to cut it down.
He laid his thongs aside and started cutting.
Finally the TREE STARTED FALLING and he RAN AWAY,
      ALL THE WAY BACK TO HIS GRANDMOTHER.
"Dear me! grandson, why did you come back so soon?"
      that's what his grandmother said.

                              •

"Well, didn't you
tell me that when I cut the tree and the tree

fell, I SHOULD RUN AWAY? AND I LEFT ALL MY
THONGS THERE." *(almost laughs)*

•

That's what he said.
"YOU BIG FOOL, YOU SHOULD'VE RUN ONLY A
    SHORT DISTANCE FROM THE TREE, THEN YOU
SHOULD'VE RETURNED to chop it up and make a bundle
and you should've brought that home on your back, that's
    what I meant, you shouldn't have run all the way home."
"Why did you have to give me INSTRUCTIONS?
But anyway
let's eat, then I'll go back to make a bundle of wood and
    then come back here," he said.
When they had eaten: "Well, I'm going."
Then the boy went on his way until
he came to where he had cut the tree, then he made a
    bundle of wood. When he had finished the bundle he
    cut some juniper leaves.
He put these
on his back where the load was going to rest, then
    put the bundle there

•

and started on his way, going short distances and then
    resting. He went on his way until he got back to his
    house.
He loosed his bundle and
went down inside
then the two of them ate.

"Now you have learned something, I have taught you.

So now you'll be going after wood, and when you've
        cut the tree and it falls, you must watch out. You
        must run only a short distance, you
mustn't run all the way home, that's not what I told you."
        "Well, at first
I thought I was supposed to come all the way back here:
that's why I ran back. Next time, I
won't do that."
That's what the boy said. Then they slept through the night.
        They slept through the night, and the next day, he
took his bow and
over at Rockpile Mountain he went around
pulling cottontails out of their burrows. He went
        around until he had killed four cottontails,
        then brought them home.
When he got back, he and his grandmother slept
        through the night. They slept through the night,
        and the next day he went down to his
field and went about hoeing. When it was about this time
        (points almost straight up)
about noon, he went back up to eat. "I want to go
to the Middle Place."
"Please come back soon," she said
for it was already afternoon. "You must
take care of yourself."
That's what she told him.
"W-Why
why did you say that?" he said. "Well

you must be on the alert, for

without doubt, you

will be noticed by the GIRLS," she said, for HIS

VOICE WAS VERY HOARSE.

His voice was very hoarse, and he went to the well

he came to the well.

Sure enough

the girls were coming down to get their water and going back up.

"Are you coming down to get water?" that's what he

said, with his really hoarse voice.

"Yes.

•

Why don't we

go up to my house?

My, but you're cute 'n silly," that's what

the girl who came down first

said to him. "Well now, I can't

go with you, for I must

go home.

When I get there

I'll ask my grandmother, and perhaps

•

if I ask her whether I can go with you, she'll

consent, and then I'll

go with you, *(pained)* I'm so bashful I can't just

go right into a person's house," that's what he

said, making himself silly.

Then another girl came: "Who is this cute fellow here?"

"Well

I don't know, he was here when I came down and he

spoke to me.

My, but his voice is CUTE," she said.

"WHAT'S THE MATTER WITH MY VOICE?" that's what

the boy said. "Well, your voice is really cute. Let's go.

Why don't we go on up?" The one who came second said,

"I'LL TAKE HIM WITH ME," AND THEY WERE

ARGUING OVER THE BOY, the two of them

were arguing.

(tight) "But I can't go with either of you, for I must go back

to my grandmother, then

I'll ask my grandmother.

When she tells me what to do I'll go with one of you,"

that's what

the boy said. "Well, HE'S MINE, for whoever finds

something first

will be the one to take it," that's what the first

girl said. "Well now

why don't you both go back up, for I'm going home."

And then

the boy went on until

he got back to his grandmother, and when they had eaten he

questioned his grandmother:

"When I left for the village, you told me to

take care of myself, and

when I got there I

drank and then I was just standing there

when a girl came down to get water.
She wanted me to go with her, and
(pained) IS THERE SOMETHING WRONG WITH MY
    VOICE?" he said.
"Well, poor thing, you don't speak well, for your
    voice is hoarse." "So THAT'S why she was admiring me
and wanting to take me home with her.
But I didn't consent, and then another girl came
and the first one said:
'I was the first one to find him, and whoever finds
    something first will be the one to take it.'
And I told them
'Wait, wait, I must go home, then I'll
ask my grandmother
and when she tells me what to do, then I'll go with
    one of you.'
That's what I said, and so
I didn't go with either of them, that's why I've
come back," he said.
"Well

                            •

well, I will tell you this:
if a girl asks you to go
to her house
and if you go with her
then you must
(slowly) keep your bow-guard near your eyes while
    you eat," that's what his grandmother told him.

"But I'll wait:
I won't go tomorrow, instead I'll
go hunting
for cottontails
      since our food is getting low."

      "Well, it's up to you," she said
and then they
went to sleep. The next day
he got up and took his bow and

                    •

went to his usual cottontail-hunting place, going around
      until he had killed four cottontails, then he took
      them home. It was evening when he got there
and they ate and then slept through the night.
The next day he got up and
went down to his field, going about hoeing.
Around noon he came back up.
      When they had eaten he said

      "I might go
well, I might go to the village," he said. "It's up to you.
But if some
girl should want you to go with her
then don't waver in your thoughts
for it happens that a boy
(slowly) will come to have in-laws somewhere," she said.
(tight) "WHAT DO YOU MEAN BY THAT?" "Well, if you
      think of marrying a girl
and you go to live somewhere else
you must still think of me now and then:

you mustn't

forget all about me." "Well, I won't forget," he said.

And so

he left, going to his

usual place, and sat up there. Sure enough they
    were coming down

coming down to get water, and one of them

filled her dipper with water and splashed him, *(almost
    spraying)* KERSHPLASHHHHHHH, and he went around
    shivering.

"I really think you're cute, why don't we go up?" she said.

"All right, let's

go on up," and while they were there the sun went down
    and

the girl took the lead with the boy following her, the two of
    them went up.

·

When she took him

inside her house:

        "My

fathers, how have you

been passing the days?" "Happily, sit down, so you've
    come," they said.

Then they

put out a seat for him

·

and the boy sat down.

    The girl fixed a meal and they sat down to eat.
    When they sat down to eat, well then

he remembered

he remembered: "Oh, my grandmother, you gave me some
    instructions."

He took off his bow-guard and LOOKED THROUGH IT
    WHILE HE ATE.

HE WAS SITTING THERE LOOKING THROUGH HIS
    BOW-GUARD, and the householders were laughing.

    (tight) "Why are you doing that?" they said

and they were laughing.

Then their father spoke to him: *(clearing throat)*

    "Son, why are you eating that way?" "Well, because
    MY GRANDMOTHER TOLD ME

that I should eat this way, that when I ate with my in-laws

I should keep my bow-guard near my eyes, that's what
    she told me

and that's why I'm eating this way," he said. "Indeed.

    So that's what you were told," they said

and THEY COULDN'T STOP LAUGHING. When the boy
    was finished:

"I'm going out to pee," he said, and he WENT OUTSIDE
    TO PEE and

went all the way back to his grandmother.

He ran away.

He entered

    ta^{la}$_a$$_a$$_{a_a}$.

    (tight) "Dear me! grandson, why have you come?" she
    said.

(excited) "Well, YOU GAVE ME BAD INSTRUCTIONS, for
     you told me to keep my bow-guard near my eyes while
     I ate. I took my bow-guard off and I
LOOKED THROUGH IT WHILE I ATE, *(pained)* and they
     really couldn't stop laughing, and I was so embarrassed
     I came home," he said. *(clicks tongue)*
"Dear me! you big fool.
That's not what I told you, YOU'RE ONLY SUPPOSED
     TO SHADE YOUR EYES WITH YOUR
     BOW-GUARD WHILE YOU EAT, YOU'RE
     NOT SUPPOSED TO TAKE IT OFF AND LOOK
     THROUGH IT."
That's what his grandmother told him. "But I went ahead and
     TOOK OFF MY BOW-GUARD AND LOOKED
     THROUGH IT
SO I COULDN'T SEE STRAIGHT TO REACH THE
     FOOD, and that's why *(almost laughs)*

•

that's why they couldn't stop laughing, and I was so
     embarrassed I said I wanted to pee, to pee, and when I
     WENT OUT TO PEE I came back here.
"Dear me! grandson, you weren't supposed to do that, but
     to keep your bow-guard near your eyes while you ate:
that's the way the SAYING goes."
That's what his grandmother told him. "You must go back."
     "Why should I? I made a fool of myself," he said.

•

THEN HE SPENT THE NIGHT

WITH HIS GRANDMOTHER, and the next day he didn't

   go to the village.

Those girls

the ones who had wanted to take him home

came down to get water and waited for him, thinking he

   might come again, but he didn't come, and he

   still hadn't come when four days had passed, and

then

he spoke to his grandmother: "Why don't I

go back to the village?"

That's what he said. "Why not, it's

up to you, but don't

                •

(sighing) do anything

that would embarrass you," that's what she said. "No, I

   won't," he said.

                •

And then

he took his

little animal skin, which

he used as a kilt, and tied it around his waist. When he

   had tied it around, he WENT BACK to the village, and

   when

he got there, he sat at his usual sitting-place, then

   one of them came down and talked to him.

Finally the sun went down

and she took him up with her.

She took him up with her, and when
they entered her house, he greeted them:

"My fathers, how have you been passing the
days?" "Happily, our child, so you've come," they
said. "Well, she brought me, that's why I
came," he said, with his hoarse voice.
And then
the one who had brought him fixed a meal.
Then their father spoke:

•

"Put away
our child's animal," that's what
he said
that's what he said, and the boy
then remembered
his animal skin.
(low and tight) "Ee——, they can't do that, it's my kilt, and
if they roll it up what'll I do for a kilt?
I must go out to pee," he said, and THE BOY WENT OUT
AND HEADED FOR HIS GRANDMOTHER.
He ran away.
And so
he entered,

ta^{la}a_aa_{a.}

"Dear me! grandson, you big fool, what have you done
now?"
"Well, when this girl took me home with her
their father said:

'Put away

our child's animal,' and I WANTED THIS ANIMAL SKIN

OF MINE so I came back," that's what

he said to his grandmother.

"Dear me! you big fool, that's not what he meant, he was

talking about SOME MEAT TO ROAST," that's

what *(almost laughs)*

•

that's what his grandmother told him.

"You should've told me that before." "GO BACK." "Well

I'm too embarrassed to go back, it's better for

me to stay," he said

and he spent the night

with his grandmother, and some days passed, and he

didn't go back.

And when

four days had passed, he went back again, and when

he got to the well

the first one

who had talked to him

came to where he was sitting and said, "Why did you

say you were going out to pee and then

go away? We waited for you but you never came back

in," she said. "Because, when I

looked through my bow-guard while I ate

you laughed, and I was so embarrassed I left," he said.

"So that's why you left. But please don't go away again.

Let's go on up." "All right

let's go," he said
and then
the girl got her water and took him to the place he had gone
     the first time, and they went in and ate. They ate
and there was another room where the girl slept.
After a time: "Well

•

let's get some rest, for it's been a long day," that's
     what their father said. The boy was taken into the
     next room, and then
the girl made the bed and they both lay down. When the girl
had fallen asleep, he started feeling her, and then he felt
     where her breasts were, her breasts.
He touched them, such hard round lumps
that's what he felt.
(tight) "Ee——, you're swelling up
     and if you die while I'm sleeping with you I'll be
     killed for it."
AND THEN THE BOY WENT OUT AND RAN AWAY.
He ran all the way back to his grandmother, and his
     grandmother scolded him. He told her
how he had felt the girl's body.
"Dear me! you big fool, that's what we're like," that's what
     his grandmother said, and SHE SHOWED HIM HER
     BREASTS.
"WHY DIDN'T YOU TELL ME THAT BEFORE I
     WENT?"
(laughing) that's what the boy said.
They slept through the night, and a few days later he went

back. Again he was taken along

he was taken inside, and

when they had eaten

　　the two of them

lay down.

He felt her again.

But wait, before he had left home his grandmother had

　　given him instructions:

"Son

when you get married

you must look for the hills," that's what she had said.

　　　　　　　　　•

And so he had gone to get married and

　　they were lying down and when

his wife had gone to sleep:

(tight and slow) "Oh, drat! you told me

to look for the hills, and if it's steamy there I should stick

　　my peeny in, now I remember what you told me."

It was late at night when the boy walked out on his wife,

　　and then

he went up to the Badger Hills and felt around there, but

　　there wasn't any STEAMY place, he went

　　around that way until:

"OH 　　 I'm
　　 NO, 　　 going
　　　　　　　　　 back

　　you've given me the wrong instructions."

It was beginning to get light by the time he got back to his

　　grandmother's house.

As they went to bed his grandmother questioned him:

•

"For what reason did you come back?" "Well, you told me
to look for the hills, and I went over to the Badger Hills
    and went around all night looking for those hills
and you told me that where it was steamy I should stick my
    peeny in, *(tight)* but I've been all over the hills and none
    of the cracks in the rocks there are steamy, so I came
    back."
That's what
he told his grandmother.

"That's NOT what I MEANT:
HERE are the hills we have," that's what she said, his
    grandmother told him. "Well, I don't want
    to get married."
That's what the boy said, and they lived on.
He went down to his field to hoe
and somehow

one girl
found this out and went to where he was HOEING. When
    she came to where he was hoeing:

                        •

"So you've come," he said. "Yes, I've come."
That's, that's what she said.

        "All right, let's
go inside," he said
and he took her
into his house.

                        •

"My grandmother, how have you been passing the days?"

"Happily, so you've come." "Yes, I've
come," she said.
"Yes, he was down there
at his field and I spoke to him
and he brought me up here, so we came in," she said.
Then they fed her and afterwards questioned her. When
they questioned her: "Well
I want to marry this child of yours, that's why I
thought of coming here
that's why I've come
for we've
already
been together one night
when I brought him up, but for some reason he went away.
He went outside and never came back, and I
was told to come here, so I came," she said.

•

"Well, he's such a
fool, so
while you were sleeping he
felt your breasts, and when he touched them
your breasts
felt like hard swellings and he thought you might die
while he was sleeping with you, that's why he left, but
I've given him a talking to. Well, why don't you
go back together?"
that's what she said.
"All right, let's go"

that's what the boy said

then she took the boy out with her

and so

the two of them

entered upon the roads of their elders, and again she brought

him in.

After she brought the boy in

they were lying down again, and he touched her

cunt, and

it was cracked:

(tight) "Ee——, someone must've hit you with

an axe, you're badly wounded.

I was told not to go back, but I must go, this shouldn't be."

That's what the boy said, and he WENT OUT and went back

to his grandmother.

His grandmother wasn't asleep yet when he got there:

"Dear me! grandson, what's your reason for scurrying

back here?" "Well, when

my wife

was sleeping I felt her

and SOMEONE MUST'VE HIT HER WITH AN AXE, and

there's SUCH a crack.

WHEN I FOUND OUT I was afraid she'd die while I was

sleeping with her, so I came back." "Dear me!

grandson, that's what we're LIKE," that's what his

grandmother said, and his grandmother *(laughs)*

showed him her cunt. "Oh well, I didn't want to get

married anyway," that's what he said. "Why didn't you

tell me this before?" "Because it shouldn't be this way,

for we value our bodies. You're such a fool, and because you're such a fool I had to show you mine," that's what his grandmother told him. *(laughs)*

They lived on this way, and because the boy was such a fool he never got married. This was lived long ago.

Lee——semkonikya. *(laughs)*

NOTES

Narrated by Walter Sanchez on the evening of March 23, 1965, with Andrew Peynetsa, Andrew's wife, son, and two small granddaughters, and myself present. Only Walter's laughter has been noted in the translation. The performance took twenty-one minutes.

Pelt Kid: in Zuni this is "Kempewi Ts'ana," literally "Pelt Little-One"; the translation "Pelt Kid" was suggested by Andrew.

Thongs: these were for tying the wood into a bundle.

"Pulling cottontails out": this is done with a three- or four-foot stick with a barbed end, inserted into a rabbit's burrow and then twisted. Pelt Kid carried his bow in case he might get a shot at a rabbit, just as a rabbit-hunter today might carry both a gun and a stick; according to Joseph, one gets more rabbits with a stick than with a gun.

Pelt Kid's hoarse voice: Walter speaks in a hoarse voice all the time, so he was unable to use hoarseness to distinguish the quotations of Pelt Kid from the body of the story.

The well: a large, open, walk-in well. Joseph Peynetsa commented, "When I was a kid there wasn't a well like that anymore, but there were maybe three places around the village where they had faucets, where the girls went to get water with buckets. Boys would meet their girl friends there. Now, with water in the houses, they have activities like basketball games and movies where kids go and meet their boy or girl friends."

"Keep your bow-guard near your eyes while you eat": Joseph explained, "When you get married you're supposed to be bashful and eat like this," and he shaded his eyes with his left wrist, where a bow-guard would be worn. It would be impolite not to act bashful. The play on meaning in the original Zuni is somewhat different from the one in my translation: Pelt Kid is told to "tuna pikwayi" his bow-guard, which means either to "look past" or to "look through," and he mistakenly makes the latter interpretation.

"A boy will come to have in-laws somewhere": Zuni newlyweds normally take up residence with the family of the wife. Today, as in the story, the act of getting married consists of little more than a man's moving in with his wife's family.

"I'm going out to pee": such a statement is perfectly proper in mixed company and might be made by a person of either sex.

"Talaaaaa": the sound of a person descending a ladder at great speed.

"Put away our child's animal": the word for "animal" here is "wemme," which means either a fur-bearing animal or its pelt; the man was referring to the butchered carcass of an animal which had been brought in from the hunt by one of his children.

"Peeny": Pelt Kid uses "shuminne," a quaint archaism, rather than "tu'-linne," which is the normal word for penis.

"The two of them entered upon the roads of their elders": that is, they entered the lives of her parents.

THE SHUMEEKULI

Well then
there were villagers at HAWIKKU
there were villagers at GYPSUM PLACE

        •

there were villagers at WIND PLACE, these were the villages
and the priest
there at Gypsum Place
spoke of having a Yaaya, a Yaaya dance.
When the word went out, people from all the villages

        •

started gathering.
The date had been set and
they lived on.

        •

For four nights
they practiced the Yaaya.
The Yaaya practice went on, and
they were gathering:
for four nights they kept gathering.
O————n it went, until
the day came.

And the SPIRAL SOCIETY
WENT INTO SESSION, and on the eve of the ceremony
    their Shumeekuli dancers came.

              •

The Shumeekuli came

              •

and the next day was to be the day

              •

for dancing the Yaaya.
Then it was the morning of the dance.
On the morning of the dance
the villagers gathered
and then
they were
getting up to dance.
O————n they went, until, at noon, they stopped to eat, and
    when they had eaten they got up again.
They got up in the afternoon

              •

and when they had done about
two sets, there were four rings of dancers.
Then the SPIRAL SOCIETY BROUGHT IN THEIR
SHUMEEKULI
and when these were brought in, the Horned Ones were also
    brought in.
They kept on dancing this way UNTIL THEIR
White Shumeekuli came, he was brought in when
there were four rings of dancers
and all the villagers had gathered:
there was a BIG CROWD, a big crowd, and
the dance kept on.

Their White Shumeekuli
kept going around the tree. He danced around it, and for

some reason

he went crazy.

•

The people HELD ON TIGHT, but somehow he broke

through their rings and ran away.

•

He ran and ran
and they ran after him.

•

They ran after him, but
they couldn't catch him

and still they kept after him shouting as they went.

He was far ahead, the White Shumeekuli was far ahead of them.

They kept on going until

•

they came near SHUMINNKYA.

Someone was herding out there

he was herding, his sheep were spread out there when they

came shouting.

"There   goes our White   Shu meekuli, running a   way, whoever is
   out there please   help us.

CATCH HIM FOR US," that's what they were shouting as

they kept after him.

(low and tight) "Oh yes, there's a Yaaya dance today,

something must've happened."

That's what the herder said, and the shouting was getting

close.

After a time, their Shumeekuli
came into view.
He was still running.

The herder stood under a tree where he was going to pass
and waited for him, then
going straight on
the Shumeekuli headed for
the place where the herder stood.

•

Sure enough, just as
he came up

past the TREE
the herder caught him for them.

There he caught him:
the White Shumeekuli
who had run away from the Yaaya dance.

The others came to get him
and took him back.

•

They brought him back, and when they
tried to unmask him
the mask
was stuck
to his face.
He was changing over.

•

When they unmasked the young man, some of his
flesh peeled off.

•

Then, the one who had come as the White Shumeekuli
lived only four days before he died.

                              •

They LIVED ON
until, at ZUNI

                              •

when the Middle Place had become known

                              •

the date was again set for the Yaaya, and when the date had
        been set they gathered for four nights.
They gathered for practice, that's the way
they lived
and when the day of the Yaaya arrived
the villagers came together on the morning of the dance.

                              •

Again the YAAYA
dance began
and again the Shumeekuli dancers were brought in.
They were brought in and they danced properly, but then
there came one who costumed himself as the White
        Shumeekuli, and he went around
until it happened AGAIN:
he went crazy.
He struggled then, but
they held onto him.
It happens whenever somebody impersonates that one:
because of the flesh that got inside that mask in
        former times

when someone comes into the Yaaya dance as the White
    Shumeekuli
something will inevitably happen to his mind. This is what
happened, and because this happened
the White Shumeekuli came to be feared.
That's all.

NOTES

Spiral Society: a medicine society which specializes in curing convulsions; only its members may impersonate the Shumeekuli and the Horned Ones.

Shumeekuli: these wear flat face masks rather than the head-covering helmet masks worn by the impersonators of most kachinas; the face is dominated by a terraced cloud, with rain falling down the cheeks. There are six kinds of Shumeekuli: yellow, blue, red, white, black, and multi-colored. They dance inside the concentric rings of Yaaya dancers, who are not masked. Joseph Peynetsa commented, "I've never seen the White Shumeekuli, but people are afraid to come as a white one. I was always scared of these dancers. If you look at them it doesn't make you feel good. That's one dance I never did like."

Horned Ones: these have helmet masks; the "horn" is a long feather, fastened at the top of the mask and sweeping forward out over the face. They dance outside the Yaaya rings.

THE BEGINNING

PART I

Well then
this
was the BEGINNING.
At the beginning
when the earth was still soft
the first people came out
the ones who had been living in the first room beneath.
When they came out they made their villages
they made their houses a————ll around the land.
They were living this way
but it was the Sun's thinking
that this
was not right
not the way to live.
They did not offer him prayer-sticks, prayer-meal.
"Well, perhaps if the ones who live in the second room come
out, it will be good."

SO THEN

when the ones who lived in the second room came out
THEIR OZONE SMELL
killed the ones who had already come out.
All of them died

and the second people lived o————n for some years
but they did not think of anything, it was not right.
Those who lived in the third room beneath were summoned.
When they came out
when the third ones came out their ozone smell killed
   all the second ones.
Their ruins are all around the land
as you can see.
Around the mountains where there is no water today, you
   could get water just by pulling up the grass
because the earth was soft.
This is the way they lived, there at the beginning.
The Sun was thinking
that they did not think of anything.
The ones who were living in the fourth room
were needed

•

but
the Sun was thinking

•

he was thinking
that he did not know what would happen now.

The clouds, the clouds were swelling.

The clouds were getting better aaaaaaAAAAAAH THE
 RAIN CAME

fine drops came, it rai————ned, it rained and rained

it rained all night.

Where there were waterfalls

the water made foam.

Well, you know how water can make foam

certainly

it can make foam

•

certainly

that water

made suds.

It was there

where the suds were made

that the two Bow Priests

sprouted.

There the two Ahayuuta

received life.

Their father brought them to life.

They came out of the suds.

When they came out: "Aha————

so we've SPROUTED." "Yes yes."

Then they stepped forward a little and stood there.

•

"Well

what are we going to do

what will our ROAD be?"
"Well I don't know."

•

At noon
when it was about noon
their Sun Father came down
near where they stood
and stepping forward a little
he came to them where they stood.
"How, father, how have you been passing the days?" "Happily
    my CHILDREN.
Have you sprouted now?" he asked them. "Yes we've
    sprouted." "Indeed."
"What's your reason for having us sprout?
Is it because something is going to happen?
Or is it because of
a WORD of some importance, something that's going to
    be said:
is that why you
brought us to life?"
That's what the Ahayuuta asked the Sun. "YES, in TRUTH
my CHILDREN
all these, our daylight, our people
have emerged, have come. When I summoned the ones in
    the first room
they came out and stood in my daylight.
I thought of them but they never offered me prayer-meal.
They never offered me prayer-sticks.

Because of this I summoned the ones in the second
room beneath.
The first ones out
made their houses all around, made villages.

THE ^{SE}COND ONES OUT, BECAUSE OF THEIR
^OZONE SMELL
DID AWAY WITH THE FIRST ONES.
The second ones made villages when they came out.
And because I thought
'The way they are living is not what I had in mind'
I summoned the ones who lived
in the third room.
When the third ones came out their ozone smell killed
the second ones.

THE ONES IN THE ^{FOURTH} ROOM ARE STILL
^{DOWN} THERE
and because I know I will need them
I have GIVEN YOU LIFE.
You will GO INSIDE.
You will bring them out, and PERHAPS THEN
as I have in mind
they will offer me prayer-meal."
That's what the Sun
told his two children. "So.
So, is this why you brought us to life?" "Yes, this
is why I brought you to life."
"Very well inDEED.
We will TRY.

This place where they may or may not live is FAR
there in the room full of SOOT
the ones who live in the fourth room," that's what the
   Ahayuuta SAID.
When they had said it:
"Well we're GOING
our FATHER.
Have good THOUGHTS.
Whatever happens when we enter upon their roads, IT
   WILL BE," they said.
"By all means may you also have good THOUGHTS.
CERTAINLY YOU WILL BRING THEM OUT WITH
   YOU," that's what their father said. "Very well."
THE TWINS WENT ON
until they came to the place of emergence.
A hole was open there.
"Well, perhaps HERE."

                        •

THEY ENTERED.
When they entered, entered the first room
it was full of the color of dawn.
The second
room they entered
was full of yellow.

IN THE THIRD ROOM THEY ENTERED
   they could hardly make anything out.
THERE IN THE FOURTH ROOM
when they entered

IT WAS FULL OF DARKNESS, NOTHING COULD BE
    SEEN
nothing could be made out.
THEY GOT THEIR FOOTING
when they came to the bottom.

                            •

Then they went some distance
toward the west and came upon two

                            •

who perhaps LIVED there, VILLAGERS
someone was close by, a DEER
someone was going around hunting, following a DEER,
    and they met him.
He came to where they were standing:
they didn't see him until he came to where they were standing.
"Haa——, so you've come," he said. "Yes."
(weakly) "What are you doing going around here?" that's
    what he asked the two Ahayuuta.
"I'm following a deer, have you seen him?"
(tight) "Well it's full of darkness here, how could
    we see a deer? We can't see anything.
WHERE DO YOU LIVE?" they asked him.
(weakly) "This way
toward the west:
that's where we live." "Indeed.
THAT'S WHERE WE'RE GOING," that's what the two
    Ahayuuta said. *(weakly)* "Indeed.
    Well, I'll take you along."

"ALL RIGHT, BUT WE CAN'T SEE. How can we find the
way?" *(weakly)* "Even so, we can find the way quite well."
"All right, but we still can't see. Wait
let us do something," and they made CEDARBARK
TORCHES.
When they had made cedarbark torches they
made them blossom
lit them
AND THE ONE WHO HAD BEEN IN THE DARK
COULD HARDLY SEE.
"Tísshomahhá
put those things out, I CAN'T SEE," that's what he said.
"IF YOU WOULD JUST FOLLOW ME, we could go."
They put out their cedarbark torches.
He took them toward the west, they went on, went on
until they arrived at a village.
"THIS is where we LIVE."

         •

"So this is where you LIVE.
Are there
perhaps
people who live, are there people who live by the
sacred things, do they have
a house here?
Isn't there

         •

that sort of
household around here somewhere?" they said. *(weakly)*

"Well perhaps I
might know why it is that you came.
Well, LET'S GO," he said, and THEY WENT TOWARD
        THE PLAZA and entered it.

                                            •

The priest's
the Sun Priest's house was the one they approached.
They went up and entered where the Sun Priest
lived, that must have been the way it was.
They entered his dwelling.
"My fathers, my children, how have you been passing the
        days?"
"Happily, our children, so you've come.
Be seated," they said. IT WAS FULL OF DARKNESS,
        THEY WERE ALL SPITTING ON ONE ANOTHER:
        BECAUSE IT WAS FULL OF DARKNESS
THEY COULD NOT SEE
WHERE ANYONE WAS.

                                            •

THEN
the one whose house this was questioned them: "NOW
for what reason have you entered upon our ROADS?
Who might you
be?" he asked them.
"WELL, I

                                            •

I AM UYUYUWI," that's what the elder brother said.
"And I am Ma'asewi."

"Indeed.

Why are you named this way?"

"Our Sun Father

brought us to life.

Because he sent us in

we have come.

Because we must take you with us out into the daylight

BECAUSE OF THESE WORDS, because of these

   instructions, we have entered upon your ROADS."

THAT'S WHAT

the two Ahayuuta said.

"Indeed.

                              •

But even if that's what you have in mind

how will it be done?

THIS PLACE WHERE YOU SPROUTED:

DO YOU HAVE THE MEANS FOR GETTING OUT

   THERE successfully?

What is known about this?"

THAT'S WHAT HE

the Sun Priest

said to them.

                              •

"WELL

well, no," the Ahayuuta said.

"But that's why we have entered upon your roads."

That's what the Ahayuuta said. "Indeed.

But if we did this
it wouldn't be right if we went out by ourselves.
Now, THERE toward the NORTH
is our father the North Priest.
Now, why don't you summon HIM?
Perhaps he will be the one who
will know
how to get OUT.
For certainly these words have been SPOKEN.
It cannot be OTHERWISE.
And whatever you have DECIDED
SO IT WILL BE," THAT'S WHAT
the Sun Priest said, the Sun Priest. "Very well indeed.

    I'LL GO," that's what the elder brother Ahayuuta said.
He went toward the north.
He went on
until he reached the North Ocean.
A house stood there.
It stood there.

"Well perhaps
the one who lives here is home"
he said, and he went up to where the house stood and
    entered.
The North Priest was there.

       •

"My ^{FA}THERRR
    how have you been passing the days?" "Happily, my
    CHILD

so you've come, be seated," that's what he told him.
"Yes, I've
come."

"Indeed.
SIT DOWN," he told him, and he sat down.
The North Priest questioned him: "NOW
my father, child
for what reason
have you entered upon my ROAD?
You would not enter upon my road for no reason.
Perhaps it is because of a WORD of some importance
that you enter upon my road.
You must make this known to me
so that I may think about it
as I pass the days," the North Priest said.
Then the elder brother Ahayuuta said, "YES, in TRUTH
my FATHER, my CHILD

                    •

because our Sun FATHER
has instructed us to take YOU
out into his daylight
into his daylight
we came to the village there.
Because they did not know
how to get out
YOU had to be summoned
and that is why
I have come to speak with you," he said. "Indeed.

•

Indeed. Since you have in truth spoken the word, it
    cannot be OTHERWISE.
Well, WAIT A MOMENT," that's what the North Priest said.
HE ASSEMBLED HIS SACRED THINGS.
He assembled his wild seeds, all his sacred things.
"WELL I'M READY," he said. "I'm ready now, so let's
be on our way."
He took his sacred things, took his wild seeds,
    garden seeds.
Then
the Ahayuuta
took the North Priest with him.
They went on until
they came to where the younger brother was.
"My fathers, my children, how have you been passing the days?"
    the Ahayuuta said.
"Happily, so you've come now."
When the North Priest entered:
"My CHILDREN
my fathers, my mothers
how have you been passing the days?" "Happily, our father,
    sit down," they told him.

When he sat down he put down his sacred things.
When he had put down his sacred things
he questioned them, the North Priest did: "NOW
my FATHERS
my CHILDREN
for what reason
have you summoned ME?

Perhaps it is because there is something important to
    say that you have summoned me.
You must make this known to me
so that I may think about it as I pass the days."
That's what he said. "YES, in TRUTH, our two fathers
    HERE
have entered upon our ROADS.
They have spoken of taking us out into their Sun
    Father's daylight
but they do not know how.
Perhaps you might know something, since your thoughts
    are rooted in your sacred things," that's what
the Sun Priest said.
"YES, in TRUTH
my CHILDREN
even if that's what you THINK about me
I do not know how to get OUT.
Perhaps my younger brother there, the Evening PRIEST:
perhaps he would know how to do THIS.
You should summon him," that's what
                        •

the North Priest said.
The younger brother Ahayuuta said:
"I'LL GO," that's what the younger brother Ahayuuta said.
He stood up.
                        •

When he stood up: "My fathers, my children, I will go
    on the ROAD.
It might be during

•

the night or during the day when I enter upon your
    roads again."
"Very well then.
May you go happily."
The younger brother Ahayuuta went out and

•

went toward the west, going along westward until he came to
    the ocean.
A house stood there.
"Well perhaps this
is where you live"
he said

    and went up
and went inside
where the Evening Priest was.
When he went inside:
"My father, my child, how have you
been passing the days?" "Happily, my CHILD
so you've come, sit down, be seated." He sat down, sat down.
The Evening Priest asked, questioned him: "NOW
my CHILD, for what reason have you entered upon my
    ROAD?
You would not enter upon my road for no REASON.
Perhaps it is because of a WORD of some importance
that you enter upon my road." "YES, in TRUTH
our Sun FATHER
brought us to LIFE.
When he brought us to life

he spoke of our taking these villagers
the ones who live here
out into the Sun Father's daylight:
that's why he made our lives whole. We went inside
and came to the village
but they
did not know how to get out, and so
your elder brother
the North Priest was summoned
and because he did not know
and BECAUSE YOU WERE THE NEXT TO BE SPOKEN
    OF
I have come
to summon you," that's what the little Ahayuuta said.
    "Indeed.
Since you have in truth spoken the WORD
it cannot be OTHERWISE.
Well, WAIT A MOMENT," he said
and going into the next room
he readied
his sacred things, his wild seeds, garden seeds
he readied them.
"NOW
let's be on our way."
They went out and went on.
They came to where the gathering was.
When they came to where the gathering was

•

they entered:

"My fathers, my children, how have
    you been?" "Happy."
"My CHILDREN
my fathers, my elder BROTHERS
how have you been passing the days?" "Happily, my younger
    brother, sit down," that's what the North Priest said.
"Happily, be seated," they were told.
The Evening Priest sat down.
When he had put down his sacred things
put down his wild seeds, garden seeds
he questioned them:
"NOW
my CHILDREN
for what reason have you summoned ME?
Perhaps it is because of a WORD of some importance
that you have summoned me.
You must make this known to me
so that I may think about it
as I pass the days," that's what he said.
"YES, in TRUTH, our two fathers HERE
have entered upon our ROADS.
Because their Sun Father
has spoken to them of taking us out into the daylight
they have entered upon our roads
but because we did not know how to get out
your elder brother here, the North Priest
was summoned, but he did not know

and because YOU WERE THE NEXT TO BE SPOKEN OF
you were summoned," that's what

                    •

the Sun Priest said. "Indeed.
But I do not know about THIS.
Perhaps our younger brother THERE
the Coral PRIEST
perhaps he would KNOW.
Well then, you should summon him," that's what
he said.
"Well, I'LL GO," that's what the elder brother Ahayuuta said.
He went toward the coral.
He came to the Coral Ocean.
A house stood there.
"Perhaps
this is where you live"

                    •

and he went up
and entered.
The Coral
Priest was there.
"My father, my child, how have you been passing the days?"
        "Happily, my FATHER
so you've come, sit down," he said.
HE SAT DOWN, the Ahayuuta sat down.
The Coral Priest questioned him: "NOW
my CHILD
for what reason
have you entered upon my ROAD?
Perhaps it is because of a WORD of some importance that

you have entered upon my road. You would not do this
    for no reason," that's what
the Coral Priest said. "YES, in TRUTH
because our Sun FATHER
who brought us to LIFE
spoke the word
of bringing YOU out
we came inside
to the village there, but they did not know
how to get out.
Your elder brothers
the North Priest
the Evening Priest
were both summoned
but because they did not know how to get out
THEY ASKED FOR YOU NEXT
and so I am summoning you," that's what the Ahayuuta
    said. "Indeed.
Since you have in truth spoken the WORD
it cannot be OTHERWISE.
Well, WAIT A MOMENT"
he said, and he went into the next room
to assemble
his sacred things, he assembled his wild seeds, garden
    seeds.
When he was ready:
"Well, I'M READY.

•

Now let's be on our way."
THE AHAYUUTA WENT THIS WAY
the elder brother did, and
brought the Coral Priest with him.
They came to where the gathering was
and went inside: "My fathers, my children, how have you been?"
        "Happy
be seated," they said.
The Coral Priest said
        "My fathers, my CHILDREN
how have you been passing the days?" "Happily, our CHILD
be seated," they told him. He put down his sacred
        things, put down his wild seeds, garden seeds.
He questioned them: "NOW
for what reason have you SUMMONED me?" he said.
"YES, in TRUTH
our two FATHERS
have come.
Their father
the Sun
who brought them to life
spoke the word of taking us out
and ^{so they en}tered up^{on our} roads.
But your elder brothers did not have the knowledge
of how to get out
and because they did not know, YOU WERE THE NEXT
to be spoken of, and so you were the one
we summoned," that's what he said. "Indeed.

How^{ever}

I do not know about this.

But it cannot be otherwise, since you have in truth
     spoken the WORD.

Well, our younger BROTHER

the Morning Priest should be SUMMONED, for he might
     KNOW about this."

That's what

the Coral Priest said.

"Well, I'LL GO."

The younger brother Ahayuuta

standing up

approached

the east

going along until

he came to the edge

                          •

of the water, where a house stood. "Well

well perhaps that's it."

He went up to it.

When he got there

he went through the door

and the Morning Priest was there.

"My father, my child, how have you been passing the days?"

          "Happily, my FATHER

so you've COME.

Sit down," he told him.

The Ahayuuta sat down.

                          •

Then

the Morning Priest questioned him: "NOW, my father, my
        CHILD

for what reason have you entered upon my ROAD?

Perhaps it is because of a WORD of some importance that

you have entered upon my road, for you would not do this

        for no reason," that's what

the Morning Priest said to the Ahayuuta. "YES

in TRUTH

my father, my CHILD

our Sun FATHER

who brought us to life

spoke of taking THESE VILLAGERS out

all of you

and so he sent us in.

When we came to the village they did not know

how to get out.

A———ll your elder bro_{thers}

from all around

have been brought together

but because they did not know

your elder brother, the Coral Priest

NEXT SPOKE OF YOU, and so

I have come

to summon you," he said. "Indeed.

Since you have in TRUTH spoken the WORD

it cannot be OTHERWISE.

Well, WAIT A MOMENT," and

going into the next room, he gathered his sacred things,

    his wild seeds, garden seeds.

When he was ready:

"Well, I'M READY." "Very well indeed."

Going out

and going on

they came to the village.

    When they came to the village

•

they went inside.

•

There was a crowd of people.

When the Ahayuuta entered:

"My fathers, how have you been?" "Happy."

When the Morning Priest entered:

"My fathers, my CHILDREN, my elder BROTHERS

how have you been passing the days?" "Happily, our

    younger brother.

So you've come, be seated," they said.

He put down his sacred things, put down his wild seeds,

    garden seeds.

He sat down.

•

"NOW

what is your reason

for summoning ME?

You must make this known to ME.

Perhaps it is because there is a word of some IMPORTANCE

that you have SUMMONED me," that's what
the Morning Priest said.
"YES, in TRUTH
our two fathers HERE
whose father the SUN
brought them to life
came in to us
because he spoke the word of taking us out.
They came here to our village
but because no one knew how to get out
your elder brothers here

                           •

have been summoned, and even though they DID NOT
     KNOW how to get out
perhaps you might know
how to get out:
that's why we have summoned you," he said.
"Indeed.
But even if that's what you have in mind, I do not know
     about THIS.
I, least of ALL.
What about our two fathers HERE?
Perhaps they know how to do this after all," that's what
the Morning Priest said.
The two Ahayuuta said, "Well
well I DON'T KNOW.
But I will try something.
My FATHERS

my CHILDREN
PREPARE YOURSELVES," that's what they told them.
That's what they told them.

THE ONES WHO LIVED BY THE SACRED THINGS
    PUT THEIR SACRED THINGS ON THEIR
    BACKS, THEIR WILD SEEDS

ALL THE VILLAGERS WERE TOLD
    ALL THE VILLAGERS
TOLD ONE ANOTHER.
The twins took them along
and went toward the east, toward where the two of them had
    come from
and the villagers
went with them.

        •

O————n
        they went until they were almost where the
twins   side:
    had come down in
"YOU MAY REST HERE," they told them.
They put down their sacred things.

"WAIT HERE WHILE WE GO ON"
    they said.

        •

They went to the place where they had come down.
"What are we going to do?" "Well perhaps we should
MAKE THE YELLOW PRAYER-STICKS," that's what
the elder brother Ahayuuta said.

        •

"Well, we might

approach the north," that's what the elder brother
 Ahayuuta said.
"Very well."

THERE THEY COMPLETED THE YELLOW
 PRAYER-STICKS.

WHEN THEY WERE FI_{NISHED}

THERE AT THE PLACE WHERE THEY WERE GOING
 TO GET OUT

they stood up the prayer-sticks.

WHEN THEY HAD STOOD UP THE PRAYER-STICKS

a fir tree

          •

GREW there.

IT GREW UNTIL IT REACHED THE NEXT PLACE

THE THIRD ROOM

AND STOOD

sticking out there a little.

"Perhaps this will do."

          •

"Very well, indeed, perhaps this will do, perhaps it's
 sticking out a little," he said.

"Now let's go back."

Then the two Ahayuuta

having made things ready

went back to where the others were.

"My fathers, my children, how have you been?"

"Happy, our fathers, so you've COME.

Has a WAY been FOUND now?" that's what they asked
them.

"The WAY has been FOUND NOW, prepare yourselves
NOW.

Let's get on the road," that's what they told them.

They put their sacred things on their backs, their garden seeds

wild seeds.

·

"ARE YOU READY NOW?" "YES, WE'RE READY."

"Well, let's be on our way." They went on, went on until

when they came to where the twins had stood up the
prayer-sticks

a fir tree stood THERE.

It stood there:

"NOW, my CHILDREN

my fathers, my children

YOU MUST CLIMB UP THE BRANCHES UNTIL YOU
GET OUT."

That's what the twins told them. "Indeed.

Very well, this is the way it will be."

The younger brother Ahayuuta

·

went up the fir tree, he was the first to go out, and sure

enough it stuck out a little

into the third

room.

HE GOT OUT FIRST

and sat down.

They all climbed UP.

aa^{aaaah}

they stepped from branch to branch, GOING UP until
they had all come out.

When everyone was out the elder brother Ahayuuta was the
last one.

"Are they all out now?" "Yes, they're all out."
They rested nearby.

"Now we can wait here awhile," they said.

•

In the third room the twins
stood up.

"Now what will be done?"

"We will bring the BLUE prayer-sticks to life. We
must approach evening's direction"

that's what he said. "Very well indeed."

•

They approached evening's direction

and FINISHED the blue prayer-sticks.

When they had fi _{nished the} blue prayer-sticks

and stood them up

•

an aspen

•

grew there.

The aspen grew
until
it reached

the second room

and stood there.

As it stood

•

they thought, "Well, it must be sticking out a little." "Yes,
    perhaps this will do."

"Yes, let's go."

THEY WENT ON UNTIL

they came to where the others were.

"My fathers, my children, how have you been?" "Happy,
    our FATHERS.

Now

has a way been found?"

"The WAY has been FOUND NOW, prepare yourselves
    NOW," that's what they told them.

They put their sacred things

on their backs.

The twins took them along until

they came to where it stood.

The aspen stood there.

"NOW, our children, you must do as before:

you must climb up the branches until you get out."

That's what they said.

"Very well indeed."

•

They climbed up until they had ALL come out.

They let them rest nearby.

"Now what will be done?" "Well, we will

make the red prayer-sticks"

    that's what they said.

They approached coral's direction.

They finished the red prayer-sticks, and when they were finished
    they set them up on the ground.

                        •

A COTTONWOOD

                        •

stood UP.

A narrow-leafed cottonwood grew.

There in the next room

IT STOOD STICKING OUT, IT STOOD OUT INTO A
    PLACE FULL OF THE COLOR OF DAWN

full of yellow.

                        •

They went back to where the others were.

"My fathers, my children, how have you been?" "Happy,
    our FATHERS.

Has a WAY been FOUND now?"

"The WAY has been FOUND NOW, prepare yourselves
    NOW," that's what they told them.

They put their sacred things on their backs, put their
    wild seeds, garden seeds on their backs.

The twins took them along until

                        •

they came to where the cottonwood stood.

    "NOW, in order to get out,
    climb the branches until you are there."

Again they climbed out

    aaaaAAAAH until they were ALL out.

"Are they all out now?" "Yes, they're all out."
It was full of the color of dawn
a yellow room.

They let them rest nearby.

The twins said

    "NOW

what will be done?"
"Well, we must make the white prayer-sticks.
We must approach the morning," that's what
the elder brother Ahayuuta said.
They finished the WHITE PRAYER-STICKS.
WHEN THEY FINISHED THEY SET THEM
    UP ON THE GROUND.
A CANE PLANT
GREW there.
The cane plant grew UNTIL IT STOOD
    STICKING OUT
INTO THE SUN FATHER'S DAYLIGHT.
It stood there
branching.

                  •

"Perhaps this will do, for this will be the fourth time we
    go out," that's what the elder brother Ahayuuta said.

"Yes, perhaps

this will do."

Then they went back to where the others were.

                  •

"NOW, my fathers, my children, how have you been?"
    "Happy, our FATHERS.

Now

has a WAY been FOUND?"

"The WAY has been FOUND NOW, prepare yourselves

NOW," that's what they told them.

"VERY WELL." Again they put their sacred things on

their backs, their wild seeds, garden seeds

they put them on their backs.

The twins took them along

until they came to where the cane plant stood.

IT WAS STANDING LIKE AN ARROW.

"NOW YOU MUST STEP FROM BRANCH TO

BRANCH AGAIN

UNTIL WE COME OUT, OUT INTO OUR SUN

FATHER'S DAYLIGHT.

EVEN THOUGH IT WILL BE HA$_{RD}$

YOU MUST DO YOUR BEST

to look at your father

for you will hardly be able to SEE.

There in the room full of soot, when we entered upon

your roads, we could hardly SEE.

This is the way it will be with you, CERTAINLY."

THAT'S WHAT THEY TOLD THEM.

They climbed UP.

SURE ENOUGH, THE MOMENT THEY CAME OUT they

dropped to the ground.

They could not bear it.

Their eyes saw nothing.

Even so, o———n

they all came out.

"Are they all out now?" "Yes, they're all out."

•

"Tísshomahhá, my CHILDREN

YOU MUST DO YOUR BEST TO OPEN YOUR EYES."

"Yes, but it's hard."

That's the way they were, o—————n

RES_{TING} WHILE THEIR ^{EYES} GREW A LITTLE
  STRON_{GER}

until their eyes were STRONG ENOUGH

to see.

They were all looking at their Sun Father.

•

"Tísshomahhá, our FATHERS

WHAT EXTRAORDINARY PERSONS YOU ARE," that's
  what they told the twins. "Indeed?

Extraordinary persons we are NOT.

It is because of the thoughts of our Sun Father that
  we KNOW THESE THINGS.

BECAUSE OF HIS THOUGHTS WE MUST ALL GO
  ALONG NOW

for some distance

and then we will rest."

That's what they told them.

"Prepare yourselves."

They put their sacred things on their backs. The twins then

took them o—————n

going on for some distance
until they arrived somewhere, having gone a long way.

•

The Sun went down.

"NOW
we will stay here four days," he said. THEY WERE
    GOING TO STAY FOUR YEARS.
FOR FOUR YEARS THEY LIVED
where they had stopped.

•

The first year came
the second, the third
AND IN THE FOURTH YEAR
THERE WAS A RUMBLING WHERE THEY HAD
    EMERGED.
There was a rumbling.
The ones who had the sacred things said, "AHAaaa
there is someone ELSE *(dogs bark outside)*
for there is his SOUND.
You two should go and find OUT.
It must be an extraordinary person
to make this rumbling," that's what
the ones who had the sacred things said to the twins.
The twins went to the place of emergence.
WHEN THEY CAME TO THE PLACE OF EMERGENCE
THERE he SAT.
A SORCERER.
Someone UNCLEAN.

Someone DANGEROUS.

A WITCH.

•

"So———it's YOU.

What is your reason for coming OUT?

Having you in this won't be good," that's what

the Ahayuuta said. "Indeed

but that's just the way it IS.

•

I am a person with garden seeds," he said. THEY
    WERE GOING TO KILL HIM.

They were going to kill him, but he didn't want it.

"Very well, it's up to YOU.

FIRST YOU MUST KILL THIS, THEN YOU CAN KILL
    ME," he said, and he showed them

his EAR OF YELLOW CORN.

"THESE are my garden SEEDS.

Yes, the others have come OUT

but their only seeds

are the ones they came out with.

THIS KIND OF CORN SEED is not among them.

THEIR FLESH

will not be good:

THAT IS WHY

I HAVE COME OUT.

But if you are going to kill me, YOU MUST KILL THIS

THEN YOU CAN KILL ME."

That's what the sorcerer told them.

They thought about it.

When they had thought about it
they did not KILL him.
They DID NOT KILL him:
"Well, let's be on our WAY.
When we get there, we will see what happens."
They took the witch with them.
When they came to where the others were
the people looked at him, an unclean person, a dangerous person.
THEN THEY WERE NOT HAPPY, the people.

•

(sighing) "Tísshomahhá
HAVING HIM IN THIS WON'T BE GOOD," THAT'S
    WHAT THEY SAID.
"INDEED, but I live by these garden SEEDS.
These yellow ones
are my garden seeds.
Even with all the other wild
        seeds,   gar den seeds
the garden seeds by which you
grow
even so
the women's flesh will not be good.
THIS EAR OF CORN
will make their flesh heavy.

•

That's why
I have COME OUT," that's what he said.
"Indeed.
But you must live a better LIFE.

The kind of person you are now: you must not be such a
   person," that's what they TOLD him. When they had
   told him
they lived on
until the fourth day
and the sorcerer spoke:

                                    •

"NOW
you must give me one of your LITTLE ONES.
(rasping) I will WITCH him," that's what he said, the
   WITCH.
The witch.
The ones who had the sacred things were not happy.

                                    •

The House Chief
had a child.

"GO AHEAD, try this one," he said, and he GAVE UP
   HIS LITTLE ONE.
When he had given up his little one, this child
was witched.
Having been hurt
the little boy died.

                                    •

His elders
held him.

ON THE ^FOURTH^ DAY
he might return:
preparations were made
so that this might be.
Preparations were made

•

and when he had been gone
four days

•

the House Chief said to the two Bow Priests

    "You must go to the place of emergence.
Our child
whose road was ended:
you must find out why it is that this had to be."
That's what he said. They were LONELY for him
    LONELY for their little one.
The two Bow Priests
went back, it was the second time they had gone back.
WHEN THEY CAME TO THE PLACE OF EMERGENCE,
    THE LITTLE BOY WAS PLAYING THERE,
    PLAYING BY HIMSELF.
When they entered upon his road: "Tísshomahhá, our
CHILD
so you are living here, not far from us," that's what
    they said. "Yes
this
is how I LIVE.
When you return you must tell my elders
that they MUST NOT CRY
for when the time COMES
then I will enter upon their roads," that's what the
    little boy said. "Indeed."
"That is why
this happened to me.

They should not cry," that's what he told them. "Very well."
They took the word back

to where the others were and told them. "Indeed.

Then that's the way it will be hereafter."
WHEN THIS HAD BEEN SAID, the two Bow Priests
spoke to THE ONES WHO HAD THE SACRED THINGS:
    "NOW
our fathers, our CHILDREN
PREPARE yourselves NOW, we've been here FOUR DAYS"
they said.
THEY HAD STAYED FOUR YEARS.

                            •

THEY STARTED OUT FROM THERE
AND WENT ON
until they came to MOSS LAKE.
When they came
to this lake
they were still only MOSS PEOPLE.
They had tails of moss.
Their hands were webbed.
Their feet were webbed.

                            •

When they came there to Moss Lake
when the twins had brought them there:
"NOW, my CHILDREN
for a time you must settle HERE.
THE WAY YOU ARE MADE is not
suitable, it will not do," that's what the twins told them.

They sat down there.

When they had sat down

THE TWINS WASHED THEM. WHEN THEY WASHED
THEM

THEIR MOSS CAME OFF.

WHEN THEY HAD WASHED ALL OF THEM

they UNDID the webs of their hands.

They used their spearhead to undo the webs. They
CUT OFF the tails.

It seems we had testicles on our foreheads.

THEY CUT ALL THESE OFF.

THEY MADE US THE KIND OF PEOPLE WE ARE
NOW, they

completed us.

THERE AT MOSS

LAKE, WE WERE WASHED. Our ELDERS, at the
BEGINNING

were WASHED there, and that is why it is NAMED MOSS
LAKE.

THEY MOVED ON FROM THERE.

MOVING ON, THEY WENT ALONG

FOR SOME YEARS

until they came to THE PLACE WHERE THE PEOPLE
WERE DIVIDED.

COMING TO THE PLACE WHERE THE PEOPLE WERE
DIVIDED, they stayed there.

They were staying there

and because THE WITCH WAS AMONG THEM

NOT ALL OF THEM
wanted to come this way.

                              •

The Ahayuuta said to them, "NOW
my fathers, my children
now we must

                              •

TEST YOU," that's what they told them. "Indeed."
The twins sat down nearby
and they made
the CROW EGG and
the PARROT EGG.
They carried these back to where the others were.
"NOW, my FATHERS, my CHILDREN
perhaps you will be WISE:
you must choose
BETWEEN THESE TWO."
That's what
they told them.
ON THIS SIDE
in the direction where the Middle of the world would be
was the CROW EGG, BEAUTIFUL
SPOTTED with BLUE.
THE PARROT EGG WAS NOT BEAUTIFUL.

                              •

There
those who were to go in coral's direction
chose the parrot egg

                              •

and those who were to come this way chose the crow egg.

·

THERE, BECAUSE THE WITCH WAS AMONG THEM
the people were DIVIDED.
When the people were DIVIDED
those who came this way brought their crow egg
not knowing
that this would be the CROW.
They went o—————n until they came to Kachina
 Village.

WHEY THEY ^CAME TO KACHINA VIL^LAGE

·

when they came to the place where Kachina Village
 was going to be
the Ahayuuta
coming to the waters there, said:
"NOW
my children, you must cross here."
That's what they told them.

·

They crossed
with their children on their backs.

THEIR ^CHIL^DREN

TURNED INTO ^WA^TER SNAKES, ^TUR^TLES
AND ^BIT^ THEIR ^EL^DERS, HALF ^THE^ CHILDREN
 WERE ^DROPPED^
AND IT WAS NOT GOOD.

"WAIT

WAIT WAIT, BEFORE EVERYONE HAS GONE IN, YOU

YOU MUST NOT DROP YOUR CHILDREN WHEN

    THEY BITE YOU, PERHAPS IT WILL

    WORK OUT THIS WAY."

Half the people had already gone in

and when the Ahayuuta said this

            •

the others held their children firmly on their backs.

They bit and scratched, but they did not let them

    go and REACHED THE OTHER SIDE.

SOME OF THE CHILDREN WERE LEFT BEHIND

    THERE.

Leaving some behind

THEY SETTLED NEARBY.

            •

On Old People's Mountain

Molanhakto emerged.

When he emerged:

"MOLANHAKTO and SIIWILU SIYEETS'A

MUST GO ON AHEAD OF US."

The Ahayuuta spoke

instructing the people that these two would go on ahead.

A SHORT DIS_{TANCE FROM} KACHINA VILLAGE

    MOUN_{TAIN}

THESE TWO

            •

SAT DOWN.
They sat down:

•

Siiwilu Siyeets'a

•

and her
elder brother Siiwilu Siwa.
As the YOUNGER SISTER
SAT THERE
sat there with her dress pulled up
her brother
became excited by his sister.
There he touched his younger sister.
It ended.
THIS BECAME THEIR SHRINE:
THOSE ^{KO}YEMSHI, IN THEIR ^{ROW}
WERE BORN THERE
AND KA^{CHINA VIL}LAGE BE^{GAN} THERE.
HALF OUR CHIL_{DREN WERE} ^{LOST} THERE
STAYED THERE, and so
it was named Kachina Village.
When THIS had HAPPENED
the Ahayuuta brought the people ON, THEY WENT ON
until they came to Hawikku.
WHEN THEY ^{CAME TO HA}WIKKU
THEY BUILT A VILLAGE.

WHEN THEY BUILT A VIL_{LAGE THERE}

when they built their FIRST village

            •

JUST _{AS THE} SUN _{HAD} WANTED IT

they offered him PRAYER-MEAL

they offered him PRAYER-STICKS:

THIS is the way it was in the BEGINNING

and THAT'S WHY

we live by the prayer-sticks.

THEY MADE THEIR VILLAGE THERE

            •

AND THE VILLAGE GREW.

SUN PRIESTS WERE MADE.

THE SACRED THINGS

were all put in place.

THIS IS WHAT HAPPENED

and a village was built at Hawikku.

            •

It happened long ago. That's all.

NOTES

Narrated by Andrew Peynetsa on the evening of March 26, 1965, with his wife, son, Walter Sanchez, and myself present. The performance took fifty-two minutes.

The rooms beneath: entire worlds under this one, numbered, like the stories in Zuni buildings, from the top down.

Ozone smell: "k'oli," the smell of lightning, or of short-circuited wires.

Ruins: the Zuni area has hundreds of ruins of Pueblo Indian villages; a few of these are attributed by the Zunis to their own ancestors, but most are not, and it is the latter to which the narrator refers.

"You could get water just by pulling up the grass": that is, the hole made by pulling up the grass would become a spring.

"The water made foam": the muddy freshets which follow rain in the Zuni area are sudsy below waterfalls because of alkaline soils.

Priests: those from the four directions, in the rank order north, west, south, east, are the human representatives of the rain-bringing Uwanammi; among priests, they are outranked only by the Sun Priest.

"Sacred things": various powerful objects possessed by a priest, among them a "sacred bundle" (mentioned in "The Hopis and the Famine") and collections of seeds. When these objects are present in a public ceremony, they are covered with blankets.

Seeds: the garden seeds (tooshoowe) referred to include, according to Andrew, corn, beans, squash, chili, wheat, peaches, pumpkins, melons, and onions; they do not include cabbage, grapes, alfalfa, and rye, "because they came in recent times." The wild seeds (kyawawulaawe) were the seeds of all wild plants found in the Zuni area.

"Your thoughts are rooted in your sacred things": Joseph Peynetsa explained this phrase as follows: "Just as orphans are dependent on their grandmother, so a priest is dependent on his sacred things."

Trees: the "fir" was a Douglas fir, and the "aspen" a quaking aspen; I am unsure of the identity of the third tree, which is "lhanil k'oha" in Zuni. "Branches" in the case of the cane plant refers to the leaves, all of which are attached to a central stem. Andrew later gave, as an alternate version of the sequence of four plants, ponderosa pine, Douglas fir, aspen, and cane.

"There was a rumbling": this was "tununu," which is the sound of an earthquake rather than the sound of thunder.

Dogs bark outside: at this precise point the dogs outside Andrew's house started barking (as if someone were coming) and continued for several lines; this, combined with the fact that it was late at night, made this part of the story even more terrifying than it would have been.

House Chief: an alternate term for the Priest of the North.

The death of the boy: this was the beginning of human death and of the afterlife. The boy came to life again after four days, but he was no longer a daylight person and could not rejoin his parents; when he said, "When the time comes I will enter upon your roads," he apparently meant that he would rejoin them when they died.

Moss People: of this episode Joseph remarked, "It sounds like evolution."

Kachina Village: the children who were lost there were the first kachinas (water snakes and turtles are alternate forms of kachinas). The boy who died before this time went back to the place of emergence, but ever since the Kachina Village episode the dead have been going to Kachina Village instead.

Molanhakto (or Siiwilu Siwa) and Siiwilu Siyeets'a: their children, the Koyemshi, were born with mental and physical defects; they are clown kachinas (not the same as the Neweekwe clowns). In English they are usually called "Mudheads," because their impersonators wear soft brown masks with lumpy facial features (including tumors).

"They built their first village": that is, Hawikku was the first village with buildings of masonry. According to Andrew, the people planted yellow corn for the first time there. He broke the story at this point "because it's an easy place to remember."

THE BEGINNING

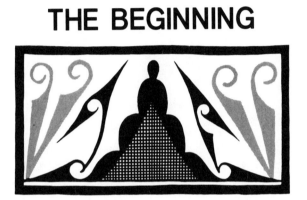

PART II

Well then

at the beginning they came to Hawikku and built a village
        there.

They built a village at Hawikku and lived on there.

•

They built their houses there. As they built their houses
the village grew, it grew.

They didn't know that the Middle Place was over here,
        so they built their village at Hawikku.

There were many people, so they constructed large buildings
        in that village. They lived on there for some years
lived on, lived on

•

until

some of them

went over to Gypsum Place and built houses there.

They built a village at Gypsum Place

and lived on there.

They went on living

and those

who had gone over to Gypsum Place lived there, but

not everyone settled there, only a few, and they were

the ones who thought of

the YAAYA

Dance: because they were wise

they created the Yaaya Dance, and it was from their

Yaaya Dance that the White Shumeekuli ran away.

When ^{this} had happened and

several YEARS had PASSED

they came

to WIND PLACE.

They came to Wind Place and built houses there.

As you can see, there were many houses

where they lived

and some way

somehow they brought in the stones, somehow they

brought in the rafters

and laid them across.

They lived on

building their houses.

They lived ^{on} there

until

when some years had passed

those

two Bow Priests

the two Ahayuuta

THOSE _{TWO}

thought:

"WHAT will be DONE about

these

our

daylight fathers, our children?

Where could they really SETTLE DOWN, pass their days

where should their VILLAGE be?

Now think about it."

That's what he told his younger brother.

His younger brother said:

"Well I DON'T KNOW.

Well

there is a————ll the wide earth

            •

and the MIDDLE PLACE might be just anywhere."

That's what they were talking about

when they thought of that water-strider.

Having thought of him

            •

they went there

to the Priest Kiva. Arriving at the House Chief's, at

    the House Chief's house, they spoke of this matter

and the priests had a meeting.

The priests had a meeting.

            •

Their Sun Priest

spoke to them:

"Well, our two fathers here

it seems

have been ^{thin}king about the lo^{ca}tion of the ^{Mid}dle Place
and by means of their thoughts we will find out
the location of this place.
Because of these two
because of their thoughts
this will be.
Not even by our combined effort
could we know
such a thing.
It is our two fathers here
who have the knowledge.

•

How else could this be DONE?
Now then, THINK about it."

•

When the priests
thought about it, they DIDN'T KNOW.
"Well, JUST AS YOU HAVE SAID
whatever these two have in mind will have to be.
IF THEY REALLY KNOW OF A DEFINITE PLACE FOR
US TO LIVE
THEN CLEARLY we should live there"
that's what
the priests said.
"Very well indeed.
I'm GOING," the twins said.
They came this way until they CAME TO ZUNI.
When they came here to the present village, they
summoned the water-strider.

WHEN THEY SUM_{MONED HIM}

he entered upon their roads.

There they spoke to him: "NOW

this very day

we have summoned you here.

              •

You

must bend over here.

YOU MUST STRETCH OUT YOUR ARMS AND LEGS.

BY THE POSI_{TION}

_{OF} YOUR HEART

the Middle Place will then become known."

That's what they said. "Indeed.

Is this your reason for summoning me?"

"Yes, this is why we have summoned you.

Now then, stretch yourself OUT.

By the position of your heart

_{IT} WILL BE KNOWN

WHERE THE MIDDLE PLACE IS," that's what

the Ahayuuta told him.

"Very well."

Bending over toward the east

he stretched out

      stretched out all his legs.

When they were ALL OUT FLAT

     WHEN THE AR_{MS}

LE_{GS}

stretched

A———LL $_A$ROUND TO THE O$_{CEANS}$

his heart

rested

at the ^{site} named the ^{MID}DLE PLACE.

　　　　　　　　　　•

They stood there:

"Very well, here is the middle

here is the middle of the EARTH"

they said, and WENT BACK.

When the two Ahayuuta had found it

　　　　　　　　　•

they went back to Wind Place, arrived at the Priest Kiva

　　　where the priests were meeting, and then they

entered:

"My fathers, my children, how have you

been?" "Happy

our fathers, so you've come, sit down," they told them.

The twins sat down.

"NOW, you have gone on the road.

When you

left you spoke of finding the Middle Place.

Has it been FOUND now?"

"IT HAS BEEN FOUND, the one who

is our child

the water-strider

$_{HAS}$ STRETCHED OUT HIS LEGS

and the site of the Middle Place has been found.
THERE
ON THE FOURTH DAY
you must go there.

·

WHEN YOU HAVE ^{GONE} THERE YOU WILL BUILD
    HOU_{SES}
you will settle a village there.
^{WHEN} YOU HAVE ^{SET}TLED A ^{VIL}LAGE THERE
when all of you have settled in that village
then we will see what happens next."
That's what the twins told them. "Very well.
This is the way it will be."

·

THERE THE AHAYUUTA TOLD THEM ABOUT THIS
and the people
told one another.
The location of the Middle Place had been found.
ON THE FOURTH DAY THEY WENT THERE to build
    their houses, they went on, went on
for some years
until the houses were finished.
When the houses were finished
^{THAT} _{WHICH IS THE} ^{HEART} _{OF THE} ^{EARTH}
    whatever it is
was thought of
by the twins.

THERE

where

the House Chief stays, there he IS, the HEART of the earth

whatever he is

perhaps a stone. (*audience member:* yes, a stone)

•

THAT'S WHERE

HE ^{I}S.

EVERYTHING

A———LL OVER THE WIDE EARTH

well

EVERYTHING DEPENDED ON HIM AND ON THE
      MIDDLE PLACE FOR FERTILITY.

FOR THEIR PART

the PRIESTS

would sit down to ask for rain.

WHEN IT ^{RAINED} AT ^{ZUNI} IT WOULD RAIN
      A———LL OVER THE $_{EARTH.}$

WHEN THEY

first started living this way

ALL the village people, at Santo Domingo

at HOPI

ALL THE VILLAGERS WOULD ANXIOUSLY AWAIT
      THE TIME

WHEN OUR PRIESTS WENT INTO RETREAT AT ZUNI,
      THE SUMMERTIME

but now
the way things are going
moisture is scarce.

.

THIS IS THE WAY IT HAPPENED
that the MIDDLE PLACE was FOUND. The MIDDLE
    PLACE was FOUND

.

AND

.

the SANIYAKYA SOCIETY
had its beginning.
JUST AS
THE ^{SA}CRED THINGS HAD ^{THEIR} BEGINNING
WHEN ^{THEY}
EMERGED
so also
the Coyote Society
the Saniyakya Society began.
THEY BE^{GAN} THERE AND CAME A^{LONG}
until they entered Kachina Village.
THERE they recited prayers.
WHEN THEY ^{ENTERED KACHINA VIL}LAGE
    they recited prayers, and today
they do the same.
THEY E^{MERGED} THERE. WHEN THE ^{SA}NIYAKYA

SOCIETY EMERGED
the YUCCA WREATH had its beginning.
THEY WENT ALONG
until they came to the Prairie-Dog Hills.
WHEN THEY CAME TO THE PRAIRIE-DOG HILLS
they had a contest with the SACRED THINGS.
WHEN THEY HAD A CONTEST WITH THE
SACRED THINGS
the sacred things
brought their heavy rain.

•

The heavy rain came, but it was NOT
like the fine rain which soaks the earth, it did
not soak the earth.
THE SANIYAKYA SOCIETY
then
sang their string of songs.
WHEN THEY SANG THEIR STRING OF
PRIESTLY SONGS
THE FINE RAIN CAME, FOUR DAYS and four nights
were filled with fine rain.
THERE
the Saniyakya Society
was singled out
as the most extraordinary, most wonderful group
at the beginning.

•

THEY BE^{GAN} THERE

and the Prairie-Dog Hills became the site of their shrine.

THAT'S WHY, AS THINGS GO TO^{DAY}

when the solstice comes
prayer-sticks are made
for the Saniyakya Society:
that is their payment.
When THIS had happened
when the sacred things
had their beginning
and the Saniyakya Society had begun
it was THEN that the
Life-Fulfilling Societies
had their beginning.

THE ^{LIFE-}FULFILLING

SOCIETIES BE^{GAN}

there in the fourth room:
some of the people were still living in the fourth
    room beneath.
When the Life-Fulfilling Societies

WHEN ^{THEY}

WERE ^{SUMMONED}

they emerged.

_EMERGING

they came out and stood in their Sun Father's daylight.

•

THEY SAW THE FOUR POLLENWAYS.

"Which one will be our road?" they said.
"We'll take the MIDDLE road
we'll go
THIS WAY, toward the east.
At Shipaapuli'ma
we will settle down together."
Ku'asaya
Iyatiiku
the White House People
Poshayaank'i:
they put
their LIFE-SEEDS in place.
Their
Bow Priests
set up shrines all around them.
The mountain lion
bear
badger
wolf
eagle
mole
set up shrines all around them.

        •

These
set up shrines.
The Life-Fulfilling Societies
sprouted their strings of songs.
WHEN THE STRINGS OF SONGS HAD SPROUTED

        •

they came to the Middle Place. When they came
to the Middle Place

•

they were placed in the room
of the priests.
When they had been put in place
then
the beasts of prey
made their strings of songs.

THERE WERE THOSE WHO SAT ^{NEA}REST, AND
THE ^{SE}COND, THIRD, FOURTH, _{THE} FIFTH
ONES, THE ^{SIXTH} ONES SAT ALL A^{ROUND}
as the strings of songs sprouted.
WHEN A ^{STRING} _{OF} SONGS _{WAS} SUNG
THOSE _{WHO SAT} NEAREST
learned the entire string.
THE ^{SE}COND ONES COULDN'T ^{GET} IT ALL
and so
that's the way it still is with the societies
as they live on.
THAT'S WHAT HAP^{PENED}:
the Life-Fulfilling Societies sprouted.
They had their beginning.
When THIS had been straightened out
ANOTHER society
then
had its beginning:
the Clown Society.

FAR OFF AT ASH ᵂᴬᵀᴱᴿ

at the spring
of the Clowns
the Clowns had their beginning.
THEY ᶜᴬᴹᴱ ᴬᴸᴼᴺᴳ
until they came to the Middle Place.

At that time
we were irresponsible.
It seems that we didn't love
our mothers
all the kinds of corn.
Our elders, our grandfathers, our grandmothers, the
    people who lived before us
DID NOT LOVE THEM, and so
the Corn Mothers ABANDONED them.
THE ᶜᴼᴿᴺ ᴹᴼᵀᴴᴱᴿˢ ₐBANDONED THEM
    and went toward the coral.
THERE ᵢₙ ᵀᴴᴱ ᶜᴼ ᴿᴬᴸ ᴼᶜᴱᴬᴺ
out in the water
a goose
nestled the ears of corn
and NO WAY
to bring them back was known.
THERE WAS NO SEED CORN.
They were living
WITHOUT SEED CORN.

They were full of anxiety.

•

Even the priests
though they were wise
did not know HOW TO GO ON LIVING.
The CLOWNS were summoned.

•

When the Clowns were summoned
Nepayatamu
came to the Priest Kiva.

•

He entered the Priest Kiva:
    "My fathers, my children, how
have you been?" "Happy, our child
sit down," they told him, and he sat down. When he sat down

•

the Sun Priest questioned him: "NOW, our father, CHILD
we have summoned you HERE.
PER^{HAPS,} AS WE HAVE IN ^{MIND}
you might
find our Corn Mothers.

•

Our Corn Mothers aren't here, they've GONE somewhere.
Because we were irresponsible
        we lost the sight of our mothers.

Since
you are an extraordinary person
perhaps
you might find them.

You might bring them back to us."
That's what they told Nepayatamu. "Indeed.

•

But even if that's what you have in mind
I don't know WHERE they WENT.

•

How—EVER
IT'S UP TO YOU," he told them.
"IF YOU WISH
then I
will look for them."

•

Then Nepayatamu told them:
"THERE WILL BE FASTING.
IF YOU WANT IT
IF YOU ARE WIL LING
to go into fasting
then I will look for them."
That's what he told them.
The priests
went to thinking.
They went to thinking.
They talked.

•

Their House Chief said
    "Well then
this is the way it will be:
WE ARE WILLING, for truly

we were irresponsible and lost our mothers, and so

we will go into fasting, we are WILLING to fast."
"IF YOU ARE WILLING TO FAST, IT MUST BE
my own sort of fast.
IF YOU FAST IN THIS WAY
THEN I WILL GO," that's what he told them.
"Yes, we are WILLING."
"ARE YOU VERY CERTAIN you are willing?"
"We are willing." "Very well indeed.
THIS VERY DAY
you will go into fasting.
THIS VERY DAY
I will go toward the coral," that's what he
    said, NEPAYATAMU.
That's what he told the priests. "Very well."

•

"Well then, I'm GOING, my FATHERS.
May you be happy as you pass the DAYS.
IF WE ARE FORTUNATE

•

it might be on the fourth
or perhaps the eighth day
when I bring them back to you. MAYbe.
PerHAPS.
CERTAINLY YOU WANT THIS," that's what he told them.
"Yes, we want it."

Then Nepayatamu went out and went toward the Coral Ocean.

•

On he went
spending three nights on the way
and after the FOURTH night he came to the Coral Ocean.
Out in the water
lay the goose.
She was nestling the ears of corn.
THERE WAS NO WAY
to get across.

•

He went about thinking
pacing up and down.
He was pacing up and down beside the waves.

•

A duck came to him.
"What are you doing?" the duck said. *(sadly)* "Well
our mothers

•

have abandoned
the Middle Place
and I'm looking for them." "Indeed.
(tight and nasal) AND YOU'VE COME HERE, but even so
what do you
plan to do?" the duck said.

•

"Well, our fathers at the Middle Place
the priests
were WILLING when I spoke of FASTING
and so I've come."
That's what
he told the duck.

"Indeed.

Very well indeed

then LET'S GO ON OUT THERE," the duck said. The duck

•

the duck

sat down in the water.

Nepayatamu sat

on the duck's back

and they flew out there

until they came to where the goose lay.

"My mother, my CHILD

how have you been passing the days?" Nepayatamu said.

"Happily, our FATHER.

So you've come," she said. "We've come."

"Indeed.

FOR WHAT REASON

have you entered upon our roads?

Perhaps it is because of a WORD of some importance

that you have entered upon our roads, for you would

not do this for no reason," that's what

the goose

told Nepayatamu. "YES, in TRUTH

my mother, my CHILD:

there at the Middle Place our fathers, the PRIESTS

have lost the sight

of their MOTHERS

all the kinds of corn.

Because they have ABANDONED us

I am looking for them." "Indeed.

BUT DO THEY REALLY LOVE THEM?" she
    asked NEPAYATAMU.

                                •

"Yes
it must be that they really love them.
WHAT THEN?"
Nepayatamu said.
"I am nestling them.
Right here I'm nestling them
but if you
have set a day for them
THEN THEY
will certainly have
that day.
Through THEIR FLESH

                                •

the women
among our daylight children
will have good flesh.
Their flesh will smell of corn."
Those
were the words of the goose.
"But if THIS is what you want
perhaps you will be very CAREFUL.

                                •

YOU ARE IN NEED
so you may GO AHEAD and take them JUST AS THEY
    ARE
and THAT will be IT.

But IF YOU HAVE DIFFICULTY on the way
then that's the way it will have to be."
Those were the words
she spoke to Nepayatamu.

"NOW
our father, CHILD
you may hold them in your arms," she told him.

.

He gathered up
ALL THE KINDS OF CORN
with his arms
locked together

.

and then Nepayatamu was FORBIDDEN to SPEAK.
"Now you must not speak
until
THE ^{CORN} MOTHERS HAVE ^{EN}TERED THE
    ^{PRIEST} KIVA

.

and have been put down together in their place.
The prayer-sticks that have been made
THE ^{PRAYER-}STICKS WILL ^{GO}

.

there
where the ones named MOLAAWE
are supposed to stay.
The prayer-sticks will enter there.
THE ^{PRAYER-}STICKS

will be put down together in their place.

•

YOU will be the one who thinks
of entering with them.
HERE^{AF}TER
this
is the ritual you will follow.
THIS IS THE WAY YOU WILL LIVE
and these are your instructions."

•

THE FASTING was held very sacred in the time
of our elders
when we were beginning to grow up.
When it was time for the MOLAAWE to come
no one made any NOISE.
No one ATE anything.
Because of this
there would be no pests, that's why
in former times
the people held their
religion
very precious.
_{BE}CAUSE THIS HAPPENED THE_N
when the Molaawe enter today
the same procedure is followed:
Nepayatamu
does not speak
when he enters

and the priests are completely quiet inside, well you
have seen this yourself, at the kiva.

                    •

When this happened, BECAUSE THIS HAPPENED THE
    CORN MOTHERS CAME BACK, and so today we
    still see
our Corn Mothers.
That, well that's all.

NOTES

Narrated by Andrew Peynetsa on the evening of March 29, 1965, with
his wife, son, Walter Sanchez, and myself present. The audience response
was from his wife. The performance took twenty-six minutes.

The water-strider: this insect is able to skim over the top of water; its four
longest legs form an equilateral cross, and in the story each of them
reaches to an ocean.

The Middle Place: noting from maps that Zuni is not equidistant from
the Arctic Ocean, the Pacific, the Gulf of Mexico, and the Atlantic, Zunis
still feel that their village must be at the center of something and they
sometimes have informal discussions as to what that something might be.
Joseph Peynetsa ventured this: "Maybe the Zunis needed a center so
they wouldn't be like the Navajos and so they would all stick together."

"The Heart of the Earth": this is never seen by the Zuni public, but it
is said to be a stone. The welfare of the entire earth is tied up in it.

The "retreat" of the priests: in the summer all the priests, one after
another, go into seclusion to pray to the Uwanammi. "Moisture is
scarce" today because the priests make mistakes.

Yucca wreath: the members of the Saniyakya Society were wearing
wreaths around their heads when they emerged; no other society uses
such wreaths.

Heavy rain, fine rain: the former, with large, splattering drops, tends to run off without soaking the earth; the latter, with small drops, may last for hours and slowly soak in.

Life-Fulfilling Societies: these are the medicine societies that stage the "Good Night" ceremony. They are modeled after the original Life-Fulfilling Society of Shipaapuli'ma, whose members are the White House People, including Ku'asaya, Iyatiiku, and Poshayaank'i. Of Ku'asaya and Iyatiiku Andrew said, "Maybe they're animals, I don't know. They're just named in the story." Of Poshayaank'i he said, "Almost like a human, but he looks like fire," and he added that he burned the timber wherever he passed on his way east.

"There were those who sat nearest": the six Life-Fulfilling Societies are ranked according to the completeness of their knowledge.

"We didn't love our mothers": that is, corn was wasted.

Corn Mothers: Joseph commented, "There must be something about those plants. In 'Dear Abby' someone wrote in that they thought a lady was crazy because she talked to her plants. Then a lady wrote that plants grow better when you talk to them. The Zunis talk to their corn. When I read that I thought, 'Well, the Zunis aren't the only ones who talk to their plants.' Then a man wrote in, sarcastic: 'What about the plants you don't want? Should you cuss them and then they'll go away?' But I don't think that would work. The Zunis go in the field, early in the morning, and sprinkle corn-meal and say, 'You, our children,' and tell them to hurry."

Duck: "eya," a mallard.

Goose: "owa," the Canada goose.

The Fasting: a period (at the winter solstice) during which it is forbidden to do business, to eat greasy foods, to take trash or ashes out of the house, or to have fire outdoors (thus the street lights are turned off and some people do not operate their automobiles). The full Fasting lasts ten days, but some people shorten its observance to eight or even four days. The "Good Night" falls on the fourth night of the Fasting.

The Molaawe: impersonators of the Corn Mothers. They come six days before the Fasting and six days after the famous Sha'lako ceremony.

About the Author

DENNIS TEDLOCK was born in Missouri and raised in New Mexico. As an undergraduate he was at the University of New Mexico, and he received his Ph.D. in Anthropology from Tulane University in 1968. Field work in linguistics, verbal art, and religion has found him among the Koasati of Louisiana, the Zuni of New Mexico, and the Quiché Maya of Guatemala. He has taught at Iowa State, Berkeley, Brooklyn, Wesleyan, The New School, and Yale, and is currently Associate University Professor of Anthropology and Religion at Boston University, where he edits *Alcheringa*, a magazine of world-wide oral poetry. In addition to the present book, he has published, with Barbara Tedlock, *Teachings from the American Earth: Indian Religion and Philosophy*.